Brooklyn
Boomer

Brooklyn Boomer

Growing Up in the Fifties

Martin H. Levinson

iUniverse, Inc.
Bloomington

Brooklyn Boomer
Growing Up in the Fifties

iUniverse books may be ordered through booksellers or by contacting:

iUniverse
1663 Liberty Drive
Bloomington, IN 47403
www.iuniverse.com
1-800-Authors (1-800-288-4677)

ISBN: 978-1-4620-1712-6 (sc)
ISBN: 978-1-4620-1713-3 (ebk)

Printed in the United States of America

iUniverse rev. date: 05/11/2011

CONTENTS

To my mother and father, the greatest of the greatest generation.
And to my wife Kathy, who encouraged me to
share my memories.

INTRODUCTION

My mother labored for forty hours, alone, before I entered the world on March 7, 1946, at the Fort Totten army hospital in Queens County, New York. My father told her when she went into the hospital, "Giving birth is no big deal. Millions of women all over the world do it each day. I'll drop by as soon as I get a chance." My grandmother was furious when she learned of my father's remarks. She said to him, "I never would have let your grandfather speak that way to me. Particularly with a first child."

Despite his sometimes gruff attitude, my father truly cared for my mother. When he proposed to her he said that she was more precious to him than his stamp collection. My Aunt Sylvia told me when she heard this story that she knew it was true love, since nothing was dearer to her brother than his stamps.

My father left the army in 1947, and our family moved to a small one-bedroom apartment two blocks from Ebbets Field, the home of the Brooklyn Dodgers. Growing up, I spent many blissful summer afternoons waiting to catch foul balls that were hit out of that ballpark. My brother and two sisters did not share my interest in baseball. What we all did share was one bedroom with four beds (mom and dad slept on a roll-away-cot in the living room). My family lived in that one-bedroom apartment for ten years and in a two-bedroom apartment in the same building for six years after that. They were among the happiest years of my life.

The following pages detail some of my recollections about living in Brooklyn during the 1950s. It also includes alternating chapters that focus on seminal cultural events of a decade that brought us the advent of television, fast-food restaurants, big cars with fins; desegregation and the white flight to the suburbs; rock and roll, beatniks, hula hoops, *The Kinsey Reports*, the Cold War, McCarthyism, and *Playboy*. Part memoir, part social history, *Brooklyn Boomer* offers an up-close and personal portrait of Brooklyn and America in the mid-20th century.

AMERICA IN THE 1950s

Some believe that life in the 1950s was an idyllic time in American history. While that may have been so for lots of white Americans, it was not the case for the majority of black Americans. Segregation and racism abounded; though there was some movement in the opposite direction, like the 1954 *Brown v. Board of Education* Supreme Court decision that ruled segregated public schools unconstitutional, there were still problems that forced blacks to fight hard for equality. Moreover, gays were wedged tightly in the closet and numerous women marked time at home when they really wanted to be out doing other things. (In *The Feminine Mystique*, Betty Friedan notes that many suburban housewives took tranquilizers like cough drops in the 1950s to dull feelings of anxiety about the pointlessness of their lives.)

But many Americans felt upbeat about the country. Discharged soldiers were attending college through the GI Bill, and after they graduated they were finding jobs in large companies, getting married, having children, buying cars, and moving to the suburbs. There, and in the cities, families gathered around the living room TV set to watch situation comedies that celebrated the virtues of family living and advertisements that hyped wondrous new products to make such living easier and better.

Most individuals trusted the government and had faith in their leaders. They also had faith in the nation's economic system, which was characterized by high levels of employment and relatively low inflation—from 1950-1958 the economy had a steady high growth rate of 4.7%. ("Never had so many people, anywhere, been so well off," the pleased-as-punch editors of *U.S. News and World Report* concluded in 1957.) And people had faith in God: a greater percentage of Americans attended church in the fifties than at any other time in US history; in 1954, Congress added the phrase "under God" to the Pledge of Allegiance and the next year mandated "In God We Trust" on all US currency.

Television and AM radio were immensely popular. Through these media, rock and roll (the music of youth, sex and rebellion) reached millions of teenagers, leading them to become freer and more independent than their parents had ever been as adolescents. Elvis Presley became a cultural icon. *American Bandstand* became the launching pad for dozens of Top-40 pop music stars.

Clothing and grooming styles evolved. Boys wore sideburns, slicked back their hair, and donned jeans and leather jackets with upturned collars to be cool. Girls sported ponytails, poodle skirts, pedal pushers, and scarves. Bigger busts and smaller waistlines a la Marilyn Monroe were all the rage.

Sock hops, hula hoops, and cruising emerged as "in" activities and kids developed their own slang, with words and expressions like *squares, chicks, going ape, be bop, back seat bingo* (kissing in the back seat), *hip* (cool), and *big daddy* (an older person). Many of the words had "ville" added to them. There was *squaresville, coolsville, weirdsville, Doodysville, deadsville,* etc.

Despite their newfound freedom and autonomy, young people for the most part still behaved and were expected to behave respectably toward adults. Females were required to comport themselves in a ladylike manner. Males were obliged to conduct themselves like gentlemen. Premarital sex was frowned upon; if a young woman became pregnant she might be sent to a special school for girls or shipped off to live with out-of-town relatives.

While changes took place throughout the 1950s, massive societal shifts didn't occur until the 1960s, a decade which saw a huge swing in ethical values, family life, race relations, and confidence in government. To some, that is why the fifties are considered an idyllic time, an era when families and social standards were basically intact and life was less complicated and more enjoyable.

LOCATION, LOCATION, LOCATION

There wasn't a more centrally located place on the planet to live and have fun than the six-story-redbrick apartment house where I resided as a child during the 1950s. Situated at 50 Lefferts Avenue, in what is now known as the Prospect-Lefferts Gardens section of Brooklyn, the building was close to just about everything a kid could want or desire.

Meeting up with my friends to play ball was a piece of cake (a home-made confection that my mother happily served them when they came by my apartment), as my buddies and I all lived on the same block. We played stickball and touch football on the street in front of 50 Lefferts and stoopball and box ball on the adjoining sidewalk. Roller-skating on a hardwood floor, accompanied by organ music playing in the background, was done at the Empire Roller Skating rink, conveniently situated a few blocks from where I dwelled. The Freddie Fitzsimmons Bowling Alley was a gutter ball's throw from the roller rink.

Going to the park was a walk in the park; Brooklyn's celebrated Prospect Park was located a measly two-and-a-half blocks from my Lefferts Avenue abode. A magnificent urban recreational area created by Central Park designers Frederick Law Olmsted and Calvert Vaux, it comprised a band shell, boathouse (with rowboats and peddle boats), bridle paths, a carousel, a playground, 13 baseball fields, tennis courts, picnic areas, hiking trails, a skating rink, and a 12-acre zoo with elephants, polar bears, monkeys, lions, tigers, and a pony track where kids could get rides in a pony wagon. The Brooklyn Botanic Gardens, a 52-acre garden containing over 10,000 plant varieties, more than 200 cherry trees, a Japanese hill-and-pond garden, and a rose garden wherein one could lose oneself, was adjacent to the park.

When I was in the mood to read a book, or had a class assignment that required such behavior, I'd frequently head out to the central branch of the Brooklyn Public Library, at Grand Army Plaza, a leisurely 20-minute stroll from my house. The library building, an architectural tour de force (it was landmarked in 1997) with a long staircase similar to the one in front of New York City's Metropolitan Museum of Art and a 50-foot-high entranceway flanked by two enormous gilded-relief pylons, held all the books a boy could want or imagine. When I finished my reading I sometimes meandered a few avenues over to the Brooklyn Museum, which houses one of the finest collections of Egyptian art in the world and is the second largest art museum in New York City.

If I had a yen to take in a game of professional baseball I could walk three blocks to Ebbets Field, the home of the Brooklyn Dodgers, to watch "dem Bums" play. But as I was a New York Giants fan (a choice made in deference to my father who since his early days in the Bronx had rooted for Brooklyn's National League rivals), I rarely went to Ebbets. However, during Dodger home contests I'd occasionally trot over to Sullivan Place or Montgomery Street in the hope of snagging a foul ball that was hit out of the stadium.

On weekends, I might amble a couple of blocks from my digs to take in a double feature at the Patio Movie Theater, an art deco masterpiece with a highly gilded and ornamented auditorium and a goldfish pond in the lobby that people threw pennies into. I could also walk to the Kenmore, Astor, Rialto, and Albemarle movie theaters, air-conditioned all. (Movie theaters were one of the first places to be air-conditioned in New York. In the summer, my pals and I often chilled out inside them the entire afternoon.)

Around the corner from where I lived there was a kosher-style Jewish deli where one could nosh on Hebrew National hot dogs topped with hot yellow mustard and sauerkraut, mountain-high pastrami and corned beef sandwiches served on real Jewish rye, large-cut French-fried potatoes, homemade cole slaw, baked potato and kasha knishes, matzo ball soup, borscht (beet soup), brisket of beef, kishke (stuffed derma served with gravy), latkes (potato pancakes), and sour and half-sour pickles. The standard beverage accompaniment to a delicatessen meal was a Dr. Brown's cream, black cherry, root beer, or Cel-Ray soda. Desserts were listed on the menu but rarely ordered, because at the end of a deli feast a person was usually stuffed to the gills.

Next door to the delicatessen was Mom and Pop's Candy Store, where egg creams, malted milk shakes, cherry lime rickeys, and full-flavored vanilla and cherry Cokes were available from a soda fountain. Mom and Pop's also carried *Superman, Batman, Sgt. Rock, Dennis the Menace*, and *Archie* comic books; Topps Baseball, Wings, and Davy Crockett trading cards; Italian ices, Dixie Cups, Popsicles, and Breyers ice cream; and an assortment of New York City newspapers, among them *The New York Times, The New York Post, The Journal American, The World-Telegram & Sun, The Daily News, The Daily Mirror,* and *The Herald Tribune.*

There was a myriad of candies to choose from at Mom and Pop's and, as they were all so good and reasonably priced, selecting a particular candy was never an easy task. Nevertheless, it was a job I looked forward to because the payoff was so rewarding. The following list includes but a sampling of the sugary and seductive sweets that Mom and Pop's purveyed: Necco Wafers, Canada Mints, Jujyfruits, Skybars, Sugar Babies, Good & Plenty licorice candy, Mallo Cups, pumpkin seeds, Tootsie Roll Pops, Milk Duds, Swedish Fish, York Peppermint Patties, Jawbreakers, Chuckles jelly candy, Junior Mints, Jujubes, Candy Buttons, Mason Dots, Zagnuts, Wax Bottles, rectangular Pez confectionaries in their plastic pocket mechanical dispensers, Beer Nuts, Skittles, Red Hots, Sen Sen, Boston Baked Beans, candy corn, and Bit-O-Honey, 5th Avenue, Snickers, Almond Joy, Mounds, Pay Day, Three Musketeers, Clark, Baby Ruth, Butterfinger, and Hershey chocolate bars.

Near to the candy store was a Chinese eatery where you could get a dinner for four that featured four entrees, two from Group A and two from Group B, for $7.95. Steamed rice was the staple, fried rice you had to ask for, and all the meals came with dark, dense duck sauce and hot yellow mustard that cleared out your sinuses if you ingested too much of it.

Crosswise from the Chinese restaurant was Ebinger's Bakery, where delicious breads and pastries were sold. Ebinger's, a retail bakery chain with stores across the borough, was famous for their cakes and pies. Although their pineapple crunch and butter cream had their fans the holy of holies was the blackout cake, a chocolate layer cake named for the wartime blackouts, filled and frosted with dark fudge and dusted with chocolate cake crumbs. Ebinger's also made lip-smacking crumb buns with toppings that begged to be picked apart.

Jahn's Ice Cream Parlor was an ice cream sundae's throw from Ebinger's and the place to go for surreal and satisfying sundaes. Their *piece de resistance* was "The Kitchen Sink," the mother of all ice cream sundaes that could serve up to six. You could make a meal out of that gooey jumble of ice cream, chocolate syrup, whipped cream, maraschino cherries, and a whole bunch of other things, and when I visited Jahn's with my friends, we often did. I particularly liked going to Jahn's on my birthday, as birthday celebrants were given a regular-sized ice cream sundae for free if they showed the waiter their birth certificate.

Catching a movie in Manhattan, consuming a hot dog at Coney Island, or corralling a piece of Junior's cheesecake in downtown Brooklyn was no problem for me, as the venues for those activities were within easy commuting distance from the Prospect Park BMT subway station, suitably sited two-and-a-half blocks from 50 Lefferts, and the train fare was all of fifteen cents. The subway ride to Coney Island was especially interesting because the train ran above ground, so you could view the different neighborhoods you were passing through. While some of those neighborhoods contained better-looking houses than the ones in my own environs, none of those residences matched my building for its excellent location and the numerous things to see and do that were nearby, and I wouldn't have wanted to live anywhere else. Lucky for me, in growing up, I didn't have to.

THE 1950s: FOREIGN AND DOMESTIC CONCERNS

The Korean War

The Korean War, which began as a civil dispute between the provisional governments of North Korea and the Republic of South Korea, lasted from June 25, 1950, until a cease-fire on July 27, 1953. Although at first a civil war, the Korean conflict quickly spiraled into a proxy fight between the Western powers, led by the US and its allies, and the communist regimes of the People's Republic of China and the USSR. Politicians and reporters euphemistically labeled the Korean War a "police action," a tag greatly resented by many of the soldiers serving in Korea; they considered themselves military combatants, not cops.

Shortly after the hostilities began, President Truman fired General Douglas MacArthur, the supreme commander of US and UN forces in the Far East and a highly respected World War II hero, because of irreconcilable differences over policy—MacArthur had articulated a desire to "atomize" China to gain victory in Korea and was against negotiating with the Chinese. Truman's decision led to widespread and intense domestic public debate and sparked some to question the wisdom of the constitutional mandate requiring civilian control over the military. A number of Republicans demanded the president be impeached. Luckily for the country, MacArthur didn't press the issue of his firing. In his farewell address to a joint session of Congress he simply told the nation, "Old soldiers never die; they just fade away" and then in a hushed voice said "Good-bye." For the next two years the clash over Korea became a bloody standoff while peace negotiations dragged on.

Both sides finally agreed to an armistice. The Korean War left an estimated 33,000 American soldiers dead, 105,000 wounded, and a $50 billion hole in the US Treasury. It also left Truman with nowhere to go politically, as his dismissal of MacArthur led him to be unjustly disparaged as being soft on Communism. Truman did not run for re-election in 1952.

Though the Korean War was tolerated when it was being fought, this country couldn't wait to forget it when it was over. It's still referred to by many as "the forgotten war." More than 40 years after the Korean War began, a privately funded monument was finally erected in Washington in its honor.

Cold War Fears

Many people link the Red Scare of the 1950s with Senator Joseph R. McCarthy, a leader of "witch hunts" against "card-carrying Communists" and their "fellow travelers." But the fear was not confined to McCarthy's time in the Senate going after commies and their sympathizers, which occurred mostly from 1950-1954. Anxiety and panic were pervasive in the US long before and long after McCarthy's wacky fixation with "Reds under the bed."

As early as 1945, Americans were being bombarded with Cold War rhetoric warning that: "Communism is evil, and like a disease it will infect nations throughout the world, unless we fight to contain it." "If Communism gains a foothold in the US it will be goodbye capitalism and the American way of life, hello socialism and forced dictatorship." "The final, all-out encounter will be between communistic atheism and Christianity." And communism wasn't all the country had to worry about.

In World War II, America had created and used the most destructive weapon ever devised. In 1949, the USSR demonstrated they also had nuclear arms by testing an atomic bomb. Sudden nuclear obliteration was now a real and scary possibility.

The combined fears of nuclear annihilation and a communist conquest of the United States led to the construction of fall-out shelters in private and public buildings, take-cover drills in schools, public-service TV announcements advising what to do in case of an atomic attack, and a strong emphasis on the sanctity of the family as important ways to battle the Red foe. Obviously, a nuclear family couldn't forestall nuclear bombs from falling. But Americans could at least *feel* protected in their own homes. If every person worked hard to keep their family strong, and prayed hard to keep the nation safe, the "Red Menace" could be kept at bay.

McCarthyism

The term *McCarthyism* was originally coined to criticize the anti-Communist rhetoric and pursuits of US senator and Cold War crusader Joseph R. McCarthy in the 1950s. The expression is now used more generally to portray irresponsible, unverified allegations, as well as demagogic assaults on the character or patriotism of political opponents. Examples of 1950s McCarthyism include the speeches, investigations, and hearings of Senator McCarthy himself; the Hollywood blacklist, connected to inquiries conducted by the House Committee on Un-American Activities (one of whose members was California Representative Richard Milhous Nixon); and the various Red-chasing activities of the FBI under its pugnacious, publicity-seeking Director J. Edgar Hoover.

During the post-World War II era of McCarthyism, thousands of Americans alleged to be Communists or Communist sympathizers were hauled before government panels, committees, and agencies for hard-line questioning. At these inquests, accusations based on inconclusive or dubious evidence were often regarded as credible, and the threat levels posed by a person's real or assumed leftist links or beliefs were frequently inflated. Government workers, educators, employees of the entertainment industry, and union activists were the main targets of the anti-Communist inquiries.

McCarthyism led people to be dismissed from their jobs, have their careers ruined, and be sent to jail. These harmful results came mostly through court verdicts that would later be reversed, laws that would be deemed unconstitutional, dismissals that would subsequently be declared illegal, or extra-legal procedures that would fall into future disfavor.

McCarthyism was the subject of much debate and conflict in 1950s America. A Gallup poll done in January 1954 found that 50% of the American public supported McCarthy while 29% had a negative view of the senator. Earl Warren, the Chief Justice of the Supreme Court, said at the time that if the US Bill of Rights had been put to a vote it probably would have been defeated.

Civil Rights

America was a racist and homophobic nation in the 1950s. Blacks and gays faced segregation and second-class citizenship throughout the land. But both groups also began to make some headway in their struggle for equality.

In 1954, the Supreme Court unanimously ruled in *Brown v. Board of Education of Topeka* that segregated schools were unconstitutional. This landmark decision, overturning earlier rulings going back to *Plessy v. Ferguson* in 1896, paved the way for integration and advances in black civil liberties.

In 1955, Rosa Parks refused to give up her seat to a white passenger on an Alabama bus. Her action spurred the 381-day Montgomery bus boycott and became an important symbol in the battle for black equality. Parks also organized and collaborated with civil rights leaders, including boycott manager Martin Luther King, Jr., helping to launch him to national prominence in the civil rights movement.

In 1957, a federal district court ordered the Little Rock Arkansas school district to desegregate its schools. But instead of doing that, Arkansas governor Orval Faubus called in the state National Guard to prevent black students from entering Little Rock's all-white Central High School.

The televised images of troops using bayonets to keep black children from going into a school stunned the nation. When President Eisenhower, who was not a big fan of civil rights, asked Faubus to remove the soldiers he did. But white mobs shouting "Go home, niggers!" soon formed to take the place of the troops. Faced with this blatant defiance of federal authority, and worldwide denunciation, Ike called in elite US airborne personnel to escort the black students into the school building.

With respect to gay civil liberties, despite immense fear and discrimination, a number of homosexuals experienced an ongoing and increasing political awareness during the 1950s. Part of that understanding came from the formation of gay and lesbian organizations like the Mattachine Society and the Daughters of Bilitis, whose members were not afraid to express the need for social change. Their advocacy for equal treatment and opportunity eventually developed into a sizeable and vibrant gay rights movement in subsequent decades.

The fight over civil rights in the 1950s led many people to question some of the basic aims and values of American society. Was America truly a free nation? Was the government under the control of its people or was it the other way around? Did all Americans have equal rights as citizens? These questions, and the arguments they engendered, would lead to bitter conflicts and divisions in the "uncivil wars" of the 1960s.

THE BOYS OF SUMMER

In 1955, over one million fans in attendance at Ebbets Field witnessed the Brooklyn Dodgers finish that year's baseball season with a .641 winning percentage and capture the National League pennant. Some of the iconic Dodger players responsible for bringing that championship to Brooklyn were . . . Catcher: Roy Campanella; Infielders: Gil Hodges, Pee Wee Reese, Billy Cox, Jackie Robinson; Outfielders: Duke Snider, Carl Furillo, Sandy Amoros; Pitchers: Sandy Koufax, Don Newcombe, Clem Labine, Carl Erskine, Johnny Podres. The Dodgers went on to beat the New York Yankees, *aka* "The Bronx Bombers," four games to three in the 1955 World Series, Brooklyn's only Series victory before leaving the borough of immigrants and underdogs for LA. And when Elston Howard grounded out to Pee Wee Reese for the final out in game number seven there was pandemonium throughout Brooklyn.

Living three blocks from Ebbets Field, I was part of that pandemonium, screaming from my fifth-floor bedroom window, "Brooklyn rules! Dem Bums are de best! The Bronx, No Thonx!" And I was a New York Giants fan, of whom there were very few in my Flatbush neighborhood, where rooting for the Giants was like cheering on the Russians. However, the Dodgers' victory was Brooklyn's victory and it was celebrated across Kings County by all but the most intransigent Yankee supporters.

Prior to 1913, the Brooklyn Dodgers were known as the Brooklyn Trolley Dodgers, a name denoting the fact that the residents of Brooklyn had to duck and dodge the many trolleys that crisscrossed the borough at the turn of the century. But in 1913 the brand was shortened to Dodgers and, with the opening of Ebbets Field, a new era began for

Brooklyn baseball. Part of that era involved recruiting Jackie Robinson to play for the Brooks.

For most of the first half of the 20th century, no major league baseball team employed an African American player. That changed in 1947 when Jackie Robinson, a truly exceptional baseball talent, became the first African American to play in the majors. His joining the Dodgers symbolized a hope for a better America, an ideal that maybe we could all get along.

Other black players quickly followed Robinson into the big leagues, among them the preeminent baseball player of all time: New York Giants centerfielder Willie Mays, the legendary "Say Hey Kid" who wowed baseball aficionados far and wide with his speed, power, and fielding. Mays' incredible over-the-shoulder basket catch and throw of Vic Wertz's prodigious drive to deep centerfield in game one of the 1954 World Series is still considered the most famous defensive play in World Series history.

I spent a large part of my childhood trying to convince my friends that Willie Mays, who many baseball cognoscenti consider the greatest hardballer ever to put on a uniform, was a better ball player than Brooklyn's Edwin "Duke" Snider or New York Yankee superstar Mickey Mantle. But they would not admit this fact because they were Dodger and Yankee fans, so they pigheadedly argued with me.

In 1957, I received some outside validation for my pro-Mays position when the *New York Post* printed the following reply to a question I sent to their sports editor asking who the best baseball player around was: "Willie Mays is the best player in baseball today and if he stays healthy he may become the greatest baseball player ever to be involved with the sport." I carried a clipping of that response in my wallet for years, pulling it out whenever I felt the need to show external confirmation of the obvious, till it finally fell to shreds.

I didn't go to Ebbets Field much in the summer when I was growing up because I liked to play ball more than view it. However, when I did attend games there I enjoyed myself because the intimate configuration of that bandbox stadium put you really close to the action on the field. I particularly liked to watch the Schaefer (Beer) sign light up with an "h" for hit or an "e" for error when either of those two events occurred. I also looked forward to seeing whether any player would smack a ball against the 4-by-40-foot sign that was situated at the base of the right field scoreboard that read "Hit Sign, Win Suit."

Any player hitting that sign with a fly ball got a free suit from Abe Stark's clothing store, which was located at 1514 Pitkin Avenue in the East New York section of Brooklyn. However, due to the superb fielding of Dodger right fielders Dixie Walker and Carl Furillo, Stark awarded very few suits. When a customer pointed out to Stark that Furillo saved him from having to give away lots of suits, Stark, who later became Borough President, gave Furillo a free suit.

The Dodgers had lots of success during my boyhood years in Brooklyn—from 1947-1956 they won the pennant six times—and during the 1950s they were the class of the National League. But in 1951 the team fell victim to one of the biggest collapses in the history of baseball, one that's still talked about by baseball enthusiasts.

On August 11, 1951, Brooklyn led the National League by a whopping 13½ games over their arch nemesis, the New York Giants. However while the Dodgers went 26-22 from that time until the end of the season, the Giants tore up the opposition, winning 37 of their last 44 games, including their last seven in a row. At the end of the regular season, the Dodgers and the Giants were tied for first place, forcing a three-game playoff for the pennant.

The Giants took game one by a score of 3-1 before being blanked by the Dodgers in game two, 10-0. In the final game, Brooklyn led 4-2 in the bottom of the ninth inning and seemed to have the pennant won. But Giants outfielder Bobby Thomson hit a stunning three-run walk-off home run against Dodger pitcher Ralph Branca to secure the National League championship for New York. That home run, nicknamed the "Shot Heard Round the World," is the most famous homer in baseball history and it put an exclamation point on the Giants' dramatic season.

The 1955 Dodgers World-Series victory took some of the pain out of the 1951 Brooklyn cave-in for Dodger fans. When Brooklyn dropped the World Series to the Yankees in 1956, a series in which Yankees pitcher Don Larsen pitched the only perfect postseason game in baseball history, there wasn't a whole lot of sorrow. Dodger supporters had had their moment of triumph. And soon that's all they'd have as the Dodgers left for LA in 1957. The Giants split for San Francisco the same year.

The Dodgers' and Giants' rejection of their roots killed my love for baseball for a long time after those clubs left the Big Apple. How could teams that possessed such loving and loyal followers, who lived to see their heroes play and who revered the stadiums that they played in, simply pack up their bats and balls and run off to the West Coast? It made no sense to me. Baseball wasn't a business; it wasn't a secular enterprise. Baseball was a divinely inspired diversion that was meant to serve the masses in sacred sports cathedrals. In leaving New York to go to California the Dodgers and Giants had committed heresy. I wished a pox on both their new houses—and a special pox on Walter O'Malley, the Dodgers owner, who was the prime mover in pushing both teams out of New York.

Brooklyn Dodgers merchandise remains popular among fans these days: major league baseball estimates $9 million in sales every year, the Baseball Hall of Fame reports that Brooklyn photos and broadcasts are the museum's second biggest sellers behind the Yankees, and eBay lists close to 1,000 items a day relating to the Brooklyn Dodgers. It appears that the boys of summer, more than five decades later, are still hot stuff.

THE 1950S: SUBURBIA, SEX, AND SALES

Suburbia

At the end of World War II, many US servicemen went back to civilian employment and lots of women left their jobs to concentrate on bearing and rearing children. Marriage rates skyrocketed and the result was a huge boom in the birth rate (the US population grew 20% in the 1950s, from 150 million to 180 million). There was also a huge increase in the need for lodging to shelter the new families.

Thirteen million new homes were erected in the 1950s and 11 million of them were built in the suburbs. That latter circumstance was due in large part to the efforts of William J. Levitt, a New York-based real estate developer who constructed the largest housing development ever put up by a single builder.

Levitt created houses in an assembly-line manner, producing new homes at the rate of 150 per week. In Levittown, a planned community that he built near Hempstead, Long Island, Levitt fabricated thousands of substantially identical two-bedroom garage-free and basement-free houses on seventh-of-an-acre lots. Before the first 600 homes were finished, customers were standing in line. By 1951, Levittown and the immediate surrounding areas contained over 17,000 Levitt-constructed houses and the project had become so successful that Levitt was featured on the front cover of the July 3, 1950, issue of *Time*.

Blacks could not buy or rent houses in Levittown. The rental contract read "NOT TO PERMIT THE PREMISES TO BE USED

OR OCCUPIED BY ANY PERSON OTHER THAN MEMBERS OF THE CAUCASIAN RACE," with the clause in capital letters for emphasis. Although this section was eventually deleted, in response to a Supreme Court ruling, Levitt continued adhering to racial exclusions. He explained the reason for such bias in a 1954 *Saturday Evening Post* article: "As a company, our position is simply this. We can solve a housing problem or we can try to solve a racial problem, but we can't combine the two."

Not everyone was a fan of Levittown. Social critic Lewis Mumford called it "A low-grade uniform environment from which escape is impossible." "Is this the American dream, or is it a nightmare?" asked *House Beautiful.* John Keats questioned the whole idea of suburbia in his 1956 novel *The Crack in the Picture Window.* But these were minority views. Most individuals, after squeezing in with their in-laws during the Depression and the war, were eager for a house and a lawn to call their own. During the fifties, people flocked to the suburbs in record numbers. In 1945, 40% of American families owned their own home; by 1960 that number was 60%.

Sex

In the 1950s, women were encouraged to make themselves fabulously alluring but to withhold sex until marriage. Men were expected to take on the swinging bachelor's lifestyle, which was described in fastidious detail in *Playboy* magazine. The double standard reigned supreme.

The *Kinsey Reports*—of which there were two: *Sexual Behavior in the Human Male* (1948) and *Sexual Behavior in the Human Female* (1953)—challenged conventional fifties beliefs about sexuality, such as the notion that men enjoy sex more than women and that abstinence before marriage was a universal practice. They also grappled with subjects like incest and homosexuality, which had previously been taboo. Though the *Reports* were rather dry and scholarly, they caused shock and outrage, became huge bestsellers, and turned their lead author, a mild-mannered Indiana University biology professor named Alfred Kinsey, into a major celebrity.

During the 1950s, articles about Kinsey were featured in newspapers and magazines with nationwide circulations, such as *Time, Life, Look,*

Woman's Home Companion, Collier's, Newsweek, Redbook, and *McCall's.*
Kinsey appeared on the cover of the August 24, 1953, edition of *Time.*
An article in that issue featured this quote from two Kinsey acolytes:
"Kinsey . . . has done for sex what Columbus did for geography." Many
people credit Kinsey and his reports for liberalizing American attitudes
toward sex in the 1950s and for being key enablers to the "sexual
revolution" that took place in the following decade.

Hugh Hefner, another prominent progenitor to the sixties sex
revolution, believed that the puritan ethic was bad for the country
and that the pursuit of pleasure and material gain was what Americans
should strive for. To further this philosophy, "Hef" created and
published *Playboy*, a sophisticated men's magazine that highlighted
photos of naked, large-breasted women and articles on how to captivate
and seduce such creatures—and anyone else wearing a skirt. For many
individuals, *Playboy* offered an important corrective to the priggish,
hypercritical, and sexually conservative atmosphere of the 1950s.

(The first issue of *Playboy* was published in November 1953 and
featured nude calendar photos of Marilyn Monroe on the cover and
inside as "Sweetheart of the Month." That issue sold far more copies
than the media experts of the time had predicted it would. The second
issue of *Playboy* sold even more copies than the first.)

Margaret Sanger, a woman *Time* named as one of the hundred
most important people of the twentieth century, was president of the
International Planned Parenthood Federation from 1952-1959 and an
early power behind the Pill. Throughout the fifties she championed
research into birth control medication, and in 1960 her support was
vindicated when Searle received FDA approval to sell Enovid as an oral
contraceptive. The birth control pill became the most famous symbol
of the Sexual Revolution and Sanger went on to become an iconic
figure for the American reproductive rights movement.

Sales

Consumer surveys done in the 1950s showed the American public
could be influenced into buying products through psychological
manipulation. Vance Packard's 1957 bestseller *The Hidden Persuaders*
described how motivational researchers provided data to help
businesses do such emotional finessing. Through that data, companies

redesigned packages to take into account the psychological effects of color and developed advertising that included appeals to such powerful subconscious motivators as sexual desire, the fear of growing old, and the need for security. One ad executive, commenting on why consumers paid extra money for products that promised something above just functional use, said, "The cosmetic manufacturers are not selling lanolin, they are selling hope . . . . We no longer buy oranges, we buy vitality. We do not buy just an auto, we buy prestige."

A great deal of money was spent on advertising in the 1950s, more each year as the decade went on. Much of the money budgeted for advertising went to commercials on television. Some of those ads featured jingles and catchphrases that have evolved into advertising classics: e.g., "Progress is our most important product (GE)," "You'll wonder where the yellow went, when you brush your teeth with Pepsodent," "Plop, plop, fizz, fizz, oh what a relief it is (Alka Seltzer)." By 1960, TV had become the chief medium of national advertising.

Businesses used testimonials from TV celebrities, such as Ronald Reagan for General Electric and Jack Benny for Jell-O, to sell their products. Corporations sponsored entire series, with the company name featured prominently in the show's title, e.g., *The Colgate Comedy Hour*, *Kraft Television Theatre*, and the *Gillette Cavalcade of Stars*. Professional football established the "two-minute warning" in the last quarter of football games to make room for TV spots. By the close of the 1950s, two of every ten broadcasting minutes was being devoted to the promotion of goods and services.

Concerns about offending potential customers led sponsors to exert huge pressure over programming content. For example, when playwright Reginald Rose proposed doing a screenplay about racial bigotry to CBS's *Studio One*, the show's sponsor green-lighted the notion, but only with the proviso that Rose make the black family "something else" (the fear was that southern whites might be upset). In the TV show *Man Against Crime*, the program's sponsor, Camel cigarettes, came up with guidelines that the criminals were not to be shown smoking, and the protagonist could not investigate arson cases because viewers might think about the linkage between cigarettes and fires.

Companies that advertised on television were wary of drama series like the *Hallmark Hall of Fame* and *Playhouse 90* because their realistic depictions of human problems gave the lie to TV ads that claimed life's difficulties have easy answers. Such shows folded because they were not able to gain commercial support. Advertisers preferred to give their business to soap operas, games shows, and cartoon programs, the success of which moved FCC Commissioner Newton N. Minow to opine in a speech delivered at a meeting of the National Association of Broadcasters in 1961 that TV is a vast wasteland filled with boredom.

THE PLUG-IN DRUG ADDICTION

"Faster than a speeding bullet! More powerful than a locomotive! Able to leap tall buildings in a single bound! ('Look! Up in the sky! It's a bird! It's a plane! It's Superman!') . . . Yes, it's Superman . . . strange visitor from another planet, who came to Earth with powers and abilities far beyond those of mortal men! Superman . . . who can change the course of mighty rivers, bend steel in his bare hands, and who, disguised as Clark Kent, mild-mannered reporter for a great metropolitan newspaper, fights a never-ending battle for truth, justice, and the American way!"

Like millions of other kids in America who were hooked on the *Adventures of Superman* TV serial in the 1950s, I was enthralled with this strange visitor from another planet who put his superpowers to work to battle villains in Metropolis and to help out his associates, cub reporter and photographer Jimmy Olsen and *Daily Planet* writer Lois Lane. Only the element krypton could weaken the man of steel, but when some hideous evildoer tried to use it on him he always managed to escape its deadly effects. Superman was my idol and I was deeply distressed in 1959 when I learned that George Reeves, the actor who played Superman, had shot and killed himself. That was a rotten thing for Reeves to do because, in addition to saddening his loved ones, Reeves self-murder murdered my belief in his character's superpowers.

Sergeant Preston of the Yukon was another fifties TV show I really enjoyed. This adventure series featured Sergeant William Preston of the Northwest Mounted Police and his lead sled dog, Yukon King, as they fought rogues and scoundrels in the Northern wilderness during the Gold Rush of the 1890s. Preston's staunch companion and the real star of the show, a four-legged creature who did a lot more work than that biped Preston, was the intrepid Alaskan Husky, Yukon King (who was actually a large Alaskan Malamute). Typical *Sergeant Preston* plots involved the pair assisting injured trappers, tracking down smugglers, or saving cabin dwellers from wolverines.

In January 1955, *Sergeant Preston's* sponsor, the Quaker Oats Company, launched a campaign to boost the popularity of their puffed grain cereals. They stuffed 21 million land deeds into 21 million boxes of *Puffed Wheat* and *Puffed Rice*. Each was for one square inch of land in the Yukon.

For weeks I gorged myself with *Puffed Wheat* and *Puffed Rice,* hoping that I could amass enough Yukon real estate to be able to plop down in a chair on it one day. However, I had gathered less than 20 deeds when the advertising campaign ended and the deeds were no longer included in the cereals. Sadly, I don't know what became of my Yukon land deeds; and that's too bad because, while the property went bust (the Canadian government repossessed it in 1965 when Quaker Oats failed to pay $37.20 in taxes on the parcel of land they'd bought for their promotion), those certificates have fetched up to $100 apiece on eBay.

My father and I loved to watch the *Phil Silvers Show,* aka *You'll Never Get Rich*, a comedy series starring Phil Silvers as master sergeant Ernest G. Bilko of the United States Army—service number 15042699. Unlike your typical soldier who spends lots of time thinking about military matters and how he can defend the country, Sergeant Bilko was a warrior who filled most of his hours trying to make money through various get-rich-quick schemes and promotions. Bilko, in a nutshell, was a bilker.

Bilko's subordinates (men such as Corporal Rocco Barbella, Corporal Steve Henshaw, Private Dino Paparelli, and Private Duane Doberman) often helped him with his scams, but they were just as often his dupes, ready to be taken to the cleaners. Though Bilko frequently shielded his men from external antagonists, his attitude toward his platoon was basically this: if anyone was going to "take" *his* men, it was going to be him and only him. Through it all, his underlings were intensely loyal to Bilko and would rely on him to get them out of the mishaps that they regularly became entangled in.

I think my father, who had been in the army during World War II and was a bit of a wheeler-dealer himself, identified with Bilko's rebellious attitude toward military protocol and regulations. What he didn't identify with was Bilko's screwing of the troops. My dad strongly believed that if there was any screwing to be done in organizations, it was the system that should take the hit, not the workers.

I also saw lots of western serials in the fifties, among them *The Roy Rogers Show, Gunsmoke, Maverick, Wagon Train* and *Bonanza*. My favorite of the bunch was *The Lone Ranger*, a program whose eponymous character was a masked Texas Ranger of the Old West who dashed about righting injustices with the help of his faithful Indian sidekick, Tonto, who said things like "That's right, Kemosabe," or "Him say man ride over ridge on horse."

Uniquely among cowboy TV heroes, the Lone Ranger used silver bullets as calling cards and as a reminder that life is valuable and dear and not to be thrown randomly away. But that didn't stop him from continually shooting his gun at people. This was clearly a case of cognitive dissonance, or as Tonto might have put it, "White man mixed up."

When I first started to watch TV in the early 1950s, there wasn't much to see on it, and the shows that did appear took place mostly in the afternoons and evenings. At the end of the broadcast day a test pattern showed up on the screen. Everything was in black and white, or to be more precise, assorted shades of gray. Remote control? Fuhgeddaboudit! Not invented yet. If you wanted to change a channel you had to get up off your duff and walk over to the TV to do it. Reception? It came from a large outdoor antenna that sat on the roof and it was lousy.

Advertisers loved television because people would watch almost anything, including commercials. Almost every TV show had a primary sponsor each week and to make up for the relatively low audience numbers that the small screen offered, stars were expected to be seen personally using or endorsing the sponsor's products. When Philip Morris sponsored the *I Love Lucy* show, Lucy and Desi smoked in the program's intro and the "Call for Philip Moooriiiiuuss" kid came on during commercial transitions. At the end of one *Topper* episode, Anne Jeffries, who played one of Topper's ghostly visitors, declared, "Free cigarettes are going out to injured servicemen in veterans hospitals around the country. Now, that's an industry with a heart. Smoke up boys, doctor's orders!" (Nearly half of all adults smoked cigarettes in the 1950s, attracted to the hazardous behavior by jingles such as "Winston tastes good like a cigarette should," "Light up a Lucky—it's light up time!," and "For more pleasure have a Camel.")

The person who cherished TV most in my family was my mother, who never looked at it. For her the boob tube was a total blessing, as it kept the family out of the kitchen and away from making demands on her. It gave her time to think, make plans, and prepare for the next day. Someone in our family had to do those things, otherwise we'd all have starved to death in front of sitcoms, westerns, quiz shows, and variety programs—hapless victims of the plug-in drug addiction, a powerful hi-tech dependency that claimed many unsuspecting viewers during the Golden Age of Television.

The 1950s: The Golden Age of Television

In the early 1950s, there were just four television networks: ABC, CBS, NBC, and the Dumont Television Network. Broadcasting occurred during parts of the day and typically stopped by 11pm. For the rest of the time viewers received a test pattern.

Soap operas were a very popular form of TV entertainment and were watched by millions of women each day. Sports programs were for the guys, westerns for the kids, and variety shows featuring comedians, pop music stars, opera singers, ballet dancers, and even circus acts, were for the entire family. Television offered something for everyone.

In 1953, late-night programming came to TV with the debut of *The Tonight Show* on NBC. Steve Allen was the first *Tonight Show* host and Ernie Kovacs and Jack Paar succeeded him in the 1950s. When Paar left the program in 1962, Johnny Carson took over hosting duties and became the dominant force in late-night television for the next 30 years.

Game shows, like *Beat the Clock, Truth or Consequences,* and *Concentration,* were huge TV hits. Most offered small prizes and a small measure of fame for their contestants. However, quiz programs like *The $64,000 Question* and *Twenty One* raised the ante with large cash awards. In 1958, *Twenty One* was abruptly dropped by NBC after former contestant Herb Stempel charged the show was rigged. As a result of the ensuing scandal, by the end of 1959 all the big-money programs were gone and it would be many years before they re-emerged.

Live television drama, featuring anthology series such as the *Hallmark Hall of Fame, Kraft Television Theatre,* and *Westinghouse Studio One,* had its peak in the 1950s. Teleplays, like the *Playhouse 90* productions of *The Days of Wine and Roses* and *Requiem for a Heavyweight,* were sometimes made into movies. *Climax!,* an hour-long mystery-suspense TV anthology, showed the first screen adaptation of an Ian Fleming James Bond novel (*Casino Royale*) in 1954.

Sports television programs knocked radio out of the box. Millions of fans viewed the *Baseball Game of the Week* on Saturday afternoons, and the World Series was an enormous TV attraction. People abandoned their jobs to go home and watch the Series, which was played only during the day in the 1950s. Some businesses used a lottery system or an annual rotating scheme just to make sure that there would be people who came to work when the World Series was on.

Popular sitcoms like *The Adventures of Ozzie and Harriet, Father Knows Best,* and *Leave it to Beaver* established white middle-class identity as the norm and buttressed the notion that TV programming was about stereotyping. Dad brought home the bacon and mom cooked and served it, and in situation-comedy land there were maids and other household helpers to assist the little lady with her chores. Adhering to a cookie-cutter formula, TV sitcoms demonstrated that problems could be solved and lessons could be learned in the space of a mere 30 minutes. To make the instruction more appealing, a few laughs were usually tossed in along the way.

Children's programs and the benefits they could convey to the family were highly touted selling points for TV sets. Shows like *Howdy Doody* and *Kukla, Fran and Ollie,* and half-hour live-action programs like *The Lone Ranger, Sky King,* and *Lassie* could help keep the moppets entertained while mom made dinner, did the laundry, and cleaned the house. By the mid-1950s, children's shows had found their place on Saturday morning, and by decade's end the 30-minute, once-a-week format was established.

The following timeline shows some yearly developments in postwar and 1950s TV, an era that some have labeled the "Golden Age of Television" because there were so many ground-breaking shows and ideas that set the trend for what we watch on TV today.

A Postwar and 1950s TV Timeline

1947: *Howdy Doody*, a children's series starring Buffalo Bob Smith and a bunch of marionettes, premieres live on NBC. A pioneer in children's programming, it creates the pattern for many similar shows. *Meet the Press*, the longest-running TV program in worldwide broadcasting history, begins locally in Washington, DC.

1948: Introduction of Milton Berle as the host of *The Texaco Star Theater*. "Uncle Miltie" and Texaco rule Tuesday nights for the next several years and Berle's phenomenal popularity helps TV sales to go through the roof. The *Ed Sullivan Show*, originally *Toast of the Town*, debuts. Sponsored by Lincoln-Mercury, it becomes one of TV's longest-running and most successful variety series.

1949: The first Emmy Awards are presented and broadcast on television from Los Angeles. The first telethon, benefiting the Damon Runyon Cancer Fund, is hosted by Milton Berle and lasts 24 hours. On June 24, 1949, *Hopalong Cassidy* becomes the first network western series.

1950: *What's My Line?*, the longest-running game show in the history of prime time network television, debuts. National sponsors leave radio for TV at record rates, moving *Variety* to depict the migration as "The greatest exhibition of mass hysteria in biz annals." *TV Guide* selects Lucky Strike's popular "Be Happy, Go Lucky" spot as commercial of the year. In it, cheerleaders sing, "Yes, Luckies get our loudest cheers on campus and on dates. With college gals and college guys a Lucky really rates."

1951: *I Love Lucy*, a half-hour filmed sitcom starring Lucille Ball and Desi Arnaz, is born. The show's sponsor, Philip Morris, worries that people won't be interested in a program featuring a real-life husband and wife. But people are *very* interested. *I Love Lucy* ranks first in the nation for four of its first six seasons and is the most popular TV show of the 1950s.

1952: *The Adventures of Ozzie and Harriet, I've Got a Secret,* and *Dragnet* premiere. KTLA broadcasts an atomic bomb detonation. The first political advertisements appear on American television.

1953: *The Tonight Show* begins as a local New York variety show. Dwight D. Eisenhower's inauguration is the first to be covered live on television. The initial issue of *TV Guide* is released with a photo of Lucy's baby (Desi Arnaz IV) on the cover.

1954: The Army-McCarthy hearings are broadcast "gavel to gavel" by ABC and the Dumont networks. US Senator Stuart Symington underscores the media lesson being taught at these hearings when he tells McCarthy, "The American people have had a look at you for six weeks. You are not fooling anyone." The *Miss America* Beauty Contest airs for the first time on national television.

1955: The classic western series *Gunsmoke* begins its 20-year television run. *The $64,000 Question* is launched on CBS, igniting a US game show craze. The *Mickey Mouse Club,* featuring cast members called "Mouseketeers," and *The Honeymooners,* featuring the inimitable Jackie Gleason, come to television.

1956: Chet Huntley and David Brinkley take over anchor duties of the NBC evening newscast, which is renamed The *Huntley-Brinkley Report. As the World Turns* and *Edge of Night* appear on CBS as the first half-hour American soap operas (when soaps originally made their move from radio they retained their fifteen-minute length). Black-and-white portable TV sets hit the market.

1957: Elvis makes his final appearance on *The Ed Sullivan Show. Leave it to Beaver, Perry Mason, Zorro, Maverick,* and *Wagon Train* all start. NBC introduces an animated version of its "living color" peacock logo, which appears before every NBC color broadcast along with an announcer who says, "The following program is brought to you in living color on NBC."

1958: Senator Estes Kefaufer holds congressional hearings on the rising rates of juvenile crime and publishes an article in *Reader's Digest* titled "Let's Get Rid of Tele-Violence." The scandals involving rigged network quiz shows spread, resulting in the cancellation of *The $64,000 Question* and creating mayhem within the television industry. *The Donna Reed Show* and the private detective series *77 Sunset Strip,* featuring TV's most famous valet car parker, Edd "Kookie" Byrnes, are unveiled.

1959: The Grammy Awards are first televised as part of NBC's *Sunday Showcase. Bonanza,* a 60-minute western series and the first regularly scheduled TV program presented in color, debuts on NBC. It will become the highest-rated program of the 1960s and remain on the air for 14 years. (Some *Bonanza* trivia: "Little Joe" Cartwright's middle name was Francis. Johnny Cash recorded his own version of the theme song. During *Bonanza's* first season, the guest stars were paid much more than the stars of the show because the producers didn't think that the latter were famous enough to attract viewers.)

ELEMENTARY SCHOOL
MEMORIES

During the 1950s, when I was a pupil at PS 241 in Brooklyn, formal weekly "assemblies" were held in the school auditorium. At these get-togethers, boys had to wear white shirts and red ties—if a young man forgot his tie his teacher gave him a red fabric scrap to put on. Young ladies were required to wear a specified outfit as well, but in those days girls were off my radar screen so I can't remember what they wore.

Before entering the auditorium, classes lined up in "size places." PS 241 was particularly strong on size places—a point of great annoyance to me because, by virtue of being the tallest kid in the class, I was always last to be seated when we marched into our assigned rows to find our assigned seats.

After we were seated (boys in one row, girls in the next), our principal, Mrs. Frieda R. Shprentz, a formidable and incredibly stern woman who liked to stand in the front of the room with her arms folded across her chest and a scowl plastered across her face, made various "housekeeping" announcements. Then there was usually a student performance of some sort. Choral readings, a curious sort of creative endeavor, were far too common. I was once a part of a sextet of tremulous tenors who memorized and recited the celebrated World War I poem *In Flanders Fields*, a snippet of which I recall to this day:

In Flanders fields the poppies blow
Between the crosses, row on row on row
That mark our place; and in the sky
The larks, still bravely singing, fly
Scarce heard amid the guns below.

Following the presentations our school music specialist, whose name escapes me, would sit down at the piano and we'd accompany her by singing patriotic songs, among them two full stanzas from *The Star-Spangled Banner* and a stanza from *The Battle Hymn of the Republic*. We also sang hymns such as *The Lord's Prayer*, *The Lord Is My Shepherd* and *We Gather Together* (a Dutch folk song) that were set to music. I particularly liked chanting that last hymn: "We gather together to ask the Lord's blessing; He chastens and hastens His will to make known; The wicked oppressing now cease from distressing, Sing praises to His name: He forgets not his own," although I didn't understand it and still can't make heads or tails of the lyrics.

We also sang tons of Christmas carols, even though more than half the students at PS 241 were Jewish. No one ever made a big deal of that. However, when my friends and I felt a little rebellious we would sometimes alter the words to those carols. As a result, that "Deck the hall with boughs of holly" became "Flood the mall with loaves of challah" and "The First Noel" turned into "The First Joel"—to honor my buddy Joel Bernstein.

There were lots of interruptions during the school day for money collecting. In the morning, milk and cookie money was gathered so we could consume those items at recess. In the springtime, seeds and bulbs were sold for home planting, which in my case meant flowerpots-on-the-windowsill gardening. And one day each week teachers collected envelopes from us that contained cash wedged into "student thrift account" bankbooks issued by the East New York Savings Bank. Capitalism was clearly alive and well at PS 241 in the 1950s.

Wednesday afternoons at 2 p.m. was "released time" for religious instruction. This meant if you were attending religion classes somewhere else you could depart the school premises early to go to those classes. Sadly, I was taking Hebrew school lessons at the Prospect Park Jewish Center on Tuesdays and Thursdays, so on Wednesdays I had to wait till 3 p.m. to go home. At night I'd sometimes pray to God to change my Hebrew school schedule so I could leave before regular dismissal time on religious instruction days. I also occasionally prayed to the Almighty to spare New York City from an atom bomb attack by the Soviet Union.

One Cold War fear in the 1950s was that the Russians would nuke America. To mitigate the damage if such a calamity occurred, New York City education officials, in their great wisdom, forced students and teachers to participate in "take cover" drills in school. During those exercises students crouched under their desks with their heads buried in their arms, stood motionless with their backs to windows and faces pressed against walls, and laid on floors with pieces of cloth covering their bodies. The idea was that such measures would protect us in the event of a nuclear strike. Fortunately for my classmates and me, that idea was never tested.

When I was in the sixth grade, my best friend, Howard Tooter, dared me one day to shout "Izzie" at our woodshop teacher, Mr. Broder, who was walking across the street from a pizza parlor where we were both having lunch. Never one to shirk a challenge, I screamed out that appellation and, to paraphrase a line from a popular twentieth-century vaudeville sketch, "slowly he turned and step by step, inch by inch" Mr. Broder started to advance toward us. Howard ran away but I stood my ground, hoping I hadn't said anything too offensive to my shop teacher. Not a good move!

After he whacked me across my face with an open palm, Mr. Broder shrieked, "How dare you make fun of my name! My name 'Israel' appears in the bible x times [I forget the exact number that x was but it was definitely a large one]. How many times does your name appear in the Bible?" I didn't know the answer to Mr. Broder's question and even if I did, I'm sure that the name Marty isn't found as many times in the Good Book as his name is.

Praying that he wouldn't tell my parents what I had done, I profusely apologized to my aggrieved instructor and blamed the whole incident on Howard, saying that I had no idea that I was yelling out an insulting remark and would never do anything like that again. Mr. Broder accepted my apology and said he trusted that I had learned something from the incident. I, of course, *had* learned something. I had learned that Howard Tooter was a no-good, rotten ratfink and that Mr. Broder was a nutcase who wouldn't get into trouble for hitting me because if I told my parents what had occurred they would take his side, not mine.

At PS 241, there was an intricate system of student monitors that was based on the military. There were line guards and stair guards and officers who oversaw them. There were also crossing guards who stood on the street corners next to the school and advised you when it was safe to traverse the road.

It was a prestigious thing to be in the guards and if you were appointed to their ranks you received a color-coded badge—the lowest-ranking guard's badge was silver, the sergeant's badge was green, the lieutenant's was red, and the captain's was blue. If you spoke in the schoolyard when you should have been quiet in line, ran up the down staircase, or jaywalked in the street, one of the guards might spot you and give you a Guard Report, which was noted on your Permanent Record. I didn't know what a Permanent Record was, but I knew it was something you didn't want an infraction on, since that recorded breach would follow you around forever, which is a mighty long time when you're a kid. Too bad I didn't know then what I know now. Nothing lasts forever. The only thing that's permanent in life is change.

The 1950s: "It's Gotta Be Rock and Roll Music"

A number of rhythm and blues records in the 1930s and 1940s had the words *rock and roll* in their lyrics and titles. The term was also used as black slang referring to dancing and sometimes sex. But the expression "rock and roll" didn't gain mainstream popularity until 1951, when Cleveland disc jockey Alan Freed began to play "race music" by singers like Fats Domino and Chuck Berry for a multiracial audience and label the new sound rock and roll.

Fifties rock combined elements of blues, R&B, gospel, country western, hillbilly, and boogie-woogie. There was influence from folk and jazz as well. The kids dug the music.

There's some debate about what the first rock and roll song was. *Rolling Stone* declared Elvis Presley's *That's All Right, Mama* as the initial one. But not everyone accepts that assessment. Sam Phillips, owner of Sun Records, the preeminent rock record label of the fifties, has argued that Jackie Bernstein's *Rocket 88* was the first rock song. Other sources credit *Crazy, Man, Crazy* by Bill Haley & His Comets as being numero uno. But whatever rock song one thinks was the earliest, tons more followed it and some of them were sung by the nation's first rock stars.

Among that group were rockabilly singers Elvis Presley, Carl Perkins, and Jerry Lee Lewis, who drew on their country roots to compose their refrains. In 1956, *Billboard* magazine reported that Presley had placed more songs in the Top 100 than any other artist since record charts began. Black recording artists like Chuck Berry, Fats Domino, and Little Richard, who derived their music from a rhythm and blues tradition, also became quite successful.

Doo-wop, a musical style that stresses multipart vocal harmonies and meaningless backup lyrics, was a much admired rock genre. During the beginning and middle of the decade black groups like The Platters and The Coasters dominated the doo-wop scene. As the fifties progressed, growing numbers of white singers took up doo-wop singing, creating all-white groups like Dion and the Belmonts and racially integrated groups such as The Del-Vikings and Frankie Lymon & The Teenagers. The latter group brought doo-wop countrywide exposure when they appeared on national TV in 1956 to sing their smash hit *Why Do Falls Fall in Love?*

While rock stars scored big on the charts in the 1950s, classics singers like Nat King Cole, Bing Crosby, Patti Page, Frank Sinatra, and Perry Como, and country and western crooners like Johnny Cash and Hank Williams remained in vogue. (In 1955, only twelve of the nation's top fifty songs were rock and roll.) These entertainers stayed popular because there were a sufficient number of Americans, particularly older ones, who were not partial to "that crazy new music."

On August 5th, 1957, that crazy new music got a huge boost when *American Bandstand,* a Philadelphia-based program with host Dick Clark, aired its first nationwide television show on ABC.

Bandstand ran from 3 to 4:30 in the afternoon and adolescents and preteens coming out of school dashed home as fast as they could to watch it. Each show featured record artists lip-synching their latest hits (a smart idea given the high cost of sound duplication), autograph sessions, interviews, and dancing. Dress rules on *Bandstand* were strict: No slacks or tight sweaters for the girls, coats and ties for the guys. Smoking and gum chewing were prohibited. Some kids on the program, like Kenny, Arlene, and Justine, developed their own national following.

American Bandstand introduced lots of local singers to a cross-country audience and it was one of the first TV shows to be racially integrated. The program developed into a mega-merchandising source. If a song was featured on *Bandstand* thousands of records might be sold in a week. Platters played daily could pirouette to the top of the hit parade. Performers begged and pleaded to be on the show.

Clark may not have been that well informed about the music played on his program; he was reputed to be a fan of big-band and 1940s tunes. But he had tremendous rapport with the kids, inquiring about their favorite recordings ("Rate-A-Record" was a very popular *Bandstand* segment that involved three kids listening to and then numerically rating a new song), plugging the latest dance fads (like the Stroll, the Madison, and the Shake), and commenting positively on teen fashion and teen slang. With his boy-next-door image and the gracious way in which he conducted the show, Clark was also a comforting presence to parents who felt rock and roll was the devil's own music that would lead their children to perdition.

By the end of the fifties there were signs that rock and roll was on its way out. Elvis had been drafted into the army, Chuck Berry was in jail, and Jerry Lee Lewis had been banned from the airwaves. Little Richard decided to forsake his evil ways, leaving the music business to become a preacher, and Buddy Holly, Ritchie Valens, and the Big Bopper all died unexpectedly in a plane crash. Payola scandals, which implicated key figures in the music business for illegally promoting individual acts or songs, gave further sense that rock's time was over. Dick Clark's career was nearly wrecked by a payola scandal, but he dodged trouble by selling his stake in a record company and cooperating with the authorities.

Many adults were relieved by what seemed to be the end of a bizarre, menacing, and uninhibited music era. Now they hoped that record companies would do the right thing and produce pleasant-sounding melodies sung by well-mannered clean-cut vocalists. Impelled by a desire to make money, the record companies obliged them, putting out a white-bread teen-idol sound that was essentially a variant of pop music.

The first and probably most successful teen idol was cover-artist star Pat Boone, a devout born-again Christian who sang songs made famous by singers like Fats Domino, Little Richard, and Ivory Joe Hunter. Fabian looked good but couldn't sing, which wasn't a problem as he was touted as the "Tiger Man"—a sweet and cuddly cat. Ricky Nelson, a child TV star who could sing, made his television rock and roll debut in 1957, lip-synching the Fats Domino standard "I'm Walkin'" during an episode of *The Adventures of Ozzie and Harriet*. Frankie Avalon,

Bobby Rydell, Connie Francis, Bobby Darin, Paul Anka, and Bobby Vinton also gained fame as teen idols.

Rock and roll's cultural impact was huge. Much more than just a musical style, rock and roll influenced fashion, attitudes, dress, and discourse. In addition, rock and roll may have helped the civil rights cause, because both black teens and white teens shared the experience and took pleasure in the music. Today—with golden oldies, a rock and roll hall of fame and museum in Cleveland, and rock subtypes such as psychedelic rock, progressive rock, glam rock, alternative rock, punk, and heavy metal—rock and roll lives on.

Coney Island: A Fun-lover's Paradise

"If Paris is France, Coney Island, between June and September, is the world"
—George C. Tilyou, builder of Coney Island's Steeplechase Park

You took the subway to Stillwell Avenue, stepped out onto the elevated platform, and there it was, Brooklyn's Riviera, Coney Island—the place New Yorkers went to have fun in the sun in the 1950s.

There were amusement rides everywhere and lots of roller coasters. The Cyclone (whose 100-second jaunt up and down nine hills is still considered one of the best in the world) was the biggest of the vertical droppers, followed in size by the Thunderbolt, located across from Steeplechase Park. Gravity-defying thrills could also be gotten by riding the Tornado, the LA Thompson, the Bobsled, and the Virginia Reel, which was a round car that went up and down hills. If you wanted to be tossed around some more after your roller coaster trip you could jump on The Whip, an amusement where you sat two in a car that went along smoothly until you turned the corner, when it would whirl you about. Or you could take a spin on the Bumper Cars, a level ride involving small electric cars with rubber bumpers that drivers would try to crash into each other.

There were more than two miles of beaches and a boardwalk of slanted wooden planks that created a herringbone effect and made the walkway look wider than it really was. All over the boardwalk there were rides, penny arcades, shooting and throwing concessions, and small shops that sold popcorn with melted butter, corn on the cob, and swirls of cotton candy. There were also freak shows with bearded ladies, fat ladies, midgets, and barkers; and entertainments like Fascination (a bingo-like game involving a wooden table and rubber balls), Guess Your Weight, and Skee-ball (a sport similar to bowling except it's played on an inclined lane and the player aims to get the ball to fall into a hole rather than to knock down pins; afterwards you got coupons based on your score that you could redeem for prizes such as key rings, Kewpie dolls, piggy banks, and teddy bears). The entire scene was mind-boggling and the blocks surrounding the boardwalk, which contained similar attractions, were just as amazing.

One of my favorite things to do was to stop at Nathan's Famous for a couple of hot dogs and an order of crinkle-cut French fries that were served in a bag to which you added a little salt and ketchup and shook it until it became smeared with grease. The sign above their store at Surf and Stillwell Avenues read "From a hot dog to a national habit," and while I didn't know about the rest of the country, the crowds that gathered to eat frankfurters at all hours of the day and night at Nathan's Coney Island restaurant were clear evidence to me that munching Nathan's hot dogs was definitely a New York City ritual.

Buying a combination ticket to go on the wonderfully inventive and entertaining rides that dotted Steeplechase Park was something I did regularly when I visited Coney Island. I particularly enjoyed going on the ride that the park derived its name from.

The steeplechase ride was a full-sized simulated horse race that took place on eight double-tiered steel tracks suspended about 20 to 30 feet in the air that wound their way through the park's grounds and into the white-painted, glass-enclosed "Pavilion of Fun" building. You sat atop a carousal-like wooden horse that slid along a metal rail at what seemed like g-force speeds (a sign close to the ride read "Half a Mile in Half a Minute—And Fun all the way!"). A slim leather strap that encircled your waist and fastened to the horse's mane functioned as a safety device. When the ride was over there was a winner whom everyone cheered. All the riders then got off their steeds and exited out the Blow-Hole Theater, where compressed-air wind tunnels blew up the girls' skirts and clowns ran around giving people little electric shocks. The overall effect was like something out of a Federico Fellini film.

I never got up the courage to go on the Steeplechase Parachute Jump, an attraction in which riders were hoisted in canvas seats hanging below closed parachutes to the top of a 262-foot-tall tower and then released. Their descent was slowed only by the canopy—shock absorbers on the ground, consisting of pole-mounted springs, cushioned the landing. The people I knew who went on the Parachute Jump described the experience as a whole lot of fun, except when the ride malfunctioned and they got stranded in midair or tangled in the cables. Then I imagine it was a whole lot of fear.

When you entered Steeplechase Park at the main gateway on Stillwell Avenue, you had to pass through an enormous revolving barrel. Everyone would fall down and turn over, knock into each other trying to get up, and crash down again in disarray. There was also a huge slide that deposited you on one of maybe 20 large metal discs spinning in different directions. You couldn't stand up on the discs. They kept you rolling and revolving around. It was definitely not a good idea to eat a big meal before coming to Steeplechase.

Sheepshead Bay, the community next door to Coney Island, contained the famous Lundy Brothers Restaurant, a gigantic two-story California mission-style eatery seating about 2,500 people and containing a 1,200-gallon lobster tank. It was renowned for their Manhattan clam chowder, Southern-style biscuits, blueberry pie, and fish. When our family felt the urge to have seafood, Lundy's was where we went.

Lundy's had a number of entrances and it was mobbed on Sundays. There was a no-reservations policy. You looked for a table where people were having dessert, sidled up to it, and prayed they'd get out fast. Waiters dressed in crisp white jackets and black ties took your order once you were seated. If you were really famished, that would be the Shore Dinner, which cost around six bucks and included shrimp cocktail, a cup of clam chowder, baking-soda biscuits, a salad of sliced tomatoes and onions, half a cold lobster, half a broiled chicken; French fries, home fries, or corn; and for dessert blueberry pie or apple pie with Breyers ice cream. When you dined at Lundy's you left full.

Steeplechase Park closed in 1964, an event that significantly impacted the local economy and augured the end of the major amusement park era at Coney Island. The Parachute Jump, which was subleased to small ride operators and concessionaires, shut down in 1968 and Lundy's bit the dust in 2007. Nathan's and the Cyclone are still in business but don't draw big crowds like they did in the 1950s, when the cacophony and carnival-like atmosphere of Coney Island made it the greatest amusement-going venue on the planet—a fun-lover's paradise.

My father on Lefferts Avenue

My mother holds my sister Nancy—next to her are
my brother Danny, my sister Judy, and me

Parachute jump at Coney Island
(photo by Katherine Liepe-Levinson)

The Coney Island Cyclone roller coaster
(photo by Katherine Liepe-Levinson)

Steeplechase logo grin (photo by Katherine Liepe-Levinson)

Nixon For Senate campaign literature, 1950

Twenty One host Jack Barry (center), with contestants
Vivienne Nearing and Charles Van Doren

The author playing at being a soldier, early 1950s

A Korean War Memorial

Erasmus Hall High School

Eisenhower on the campaign trial

Senator Joseph McCarthy with his chief counsel Roy Cohn (right)

Trailer-shot from *The Day the Earth Stood Still* (1951)

Ebbets Field opening day, 1913

Central Branch Brooklyn Public Library
(photo by Katherine Liepe-Levinson)

The Incomparable *Say Hey Kid*, New York
Giants Centerfielder Willie Mays

Young Elvis Presley

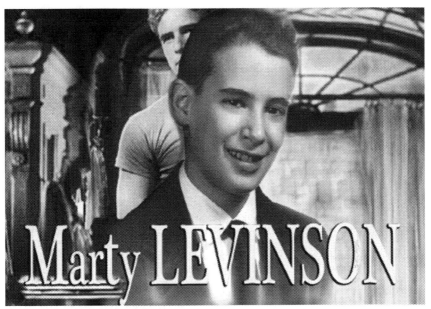

The author and Marlon Brando
(photo montage by Katherine Liepe-Levinson)

Trailer-shot of Marlon Brando in *Streetcar Named Desire* (1951)

The author at his bar mitzvah, 1959

Bill Haley and His Comets

The author in front of 50 Lefferts Avenue, 2010
(photo by Katherine Liepe-Levinson)

1959 Cadillac Seville

THE 1950s: LIVING IN A
MATERIAL WORLD

After more than a decade of a financial depression and four years of a world war that required major sacrifices in the US standard of living, Americans in the 1950s were ready to go shopping. And with lots of good-paying jobs about and relatively low rates of inflation they had plenty of money to do so. And do so they did!

Sewing machines, refrigerators, freezers, dishwashers, vacuum cleaners, ranges and ovens, washing machines, toasters, electric train sets, cars, cameras, TVs, nonstick pots and pans, portable mixers, percolators, immersible fry-pans, electric carving knives, hi-fi record players, rotisseries with see-through windows—all manner and type of consumer items flew off the shelves and showroom floors as American consumers, flush with cash and urged on by newspaper and TV advertisements, went on a decade-long shop-till-you-drop buying spree. And there were bargains to be had for the things people wanted, particularly at discount department stores, which came into their own as merchandising mega depots in the 1950s.

The EJ Korvette Company, founded in 1948, was a pioneer in the discounting field. Their low-price, low-service model was similar to that of five-and-ten-cent stores like Woolworth's and Kresge's, but Korvette's was clever in avoiding federal anti-discounting provisions and in undercutting suggested retail charges on costly items such as pricey fountain pens and appliances. The company also instituted a membership program and expanded into suburbia at a time when most discount stores were located in urban business districts. Korvette's was the model for K-Mart, Woolco, Target, and Wal-Mart, all of which began their operations in 1962.

Due to their cheap prices, wide selection, newspaper advertising, and use of trading stamps as buying incentives, supermarkets were the places to procure provender in the 1950s—retail supermarket sales rose from 35% at the beginning of the decade to 70% by 1960. When a supermarket advertised double stamp days, shoppers rocketed down the aisles with their baskets and carts to get extra stamps, which could be redeemed for merchandise at the stamp company's store or by mail. Unfortunately, when customers got to the checkout line there was occasionally a wait to exit the store; food products in the 1950s didn't have bar codes on them so each article had to be rung up singly.

Cars sold as fast as Detroit could crank them out, and new models hyped by TV, radio, and print ad campaigns debuted each year. (There were sometimes waiting lists to purchase cars, and some customers bribed dealers in order to acquire one.) American autos were big and fast, which is what buyers wanted, and dollar-for-dollar they were the best-made vehicles in the world. When Dinah Shore sang, "See the USA in your Chev-ro-lay" on the NBC-TV Dinah Shore Chevy Show her viewers didn't worry that if they decided to take cross-country excursions their Chevies would conk out.

Americans did lots of highway travel in the fifties—auto touring doubled in the US between 1950 and 1960—and many travelers chose to stay at Holiday Inns, which, with their low prices, trusty quality, and convenient locations, were like the Wal-Marts of the hospitality industry.

The Holiday Inn concept of standardized motel rooms was born in 1952 when Tennessee architect Kemmons Wilson returned to Washington, DC from a family road trip. Dissatisfied by the quality and consistency offered by the roadside motels that he stayed at, within a year, Wilson had blueprints drawn from rough sketches that he made. Those drawings were swiftly implemented, and Holiday Inns sprung up like Topsy. The notion that each room in every motel should look pretty much like any other room became the norm for Best Western, Ramada, and all the other motel chains.

People paid for what they bought in the fifties by cash or by check. However, individuals who had Diners Club cards could charge their purchases at restaurants, hotels, and other commercial establishments (the first credit card charge was made on February 8, 1950, by Frank McNamara, Ralph Schneider, and Matty Simmons at Major's Cabin Grill, a restaurant adjacent to their offices in the Empire State Building). Payment in full was expected at the end of the month. In 1958, American Express also began to issue charge cards and Bank of America came out with the BankAmericard, which allowed the option of delayed payment for goods and services. And so, for better or worse, modern consumer credit was born.

At the start of the 1950s, the National Restaurant Association endorsed a new kind of dinner called the "take home" meal—a repast requiring no preparation. Many fast food outlets emerged in the 1950s as well. The first Dunkin' Donuts debuted in 1950, Church's Chicken premiered in 1952, and the initial Burger King restaurant opened in 1954. McDonald's in the incarnation that we now know it began in 1955, as did Kentucky Fried Chicken. Pizza Hut opened for business in 1958. Eating fast food would go on to become a national phenomenon. So would watching television.

TV sets were considered an expensive extra in the early fifties but that changed as the decade progressed and as the economy kept improving. With the launch of color TV in 1954, traditional black-and-white sets became more affordable and more and more families began to buy them. By the end of 1959, nearly 90 million households had television sets, compared to about 9 million in 1950.

Swanson TV Dinners were almost as popular as TVs. Introduced by the Swanson Company in 1953, these individual-sized packaged frozen meals were housed in an aluminum tray that could be heated in the oven. The original TV Dinner cost 98 cents and had a production estimate of 5,000 dinners for the first year. However, Swanson far surpassed its expectations and wound up selling more than 10 million TV dinners in that time period; many of them were consumed by people watching television using portable, fold-away, over-the-knees TV tables to eat their food. In 1960, Swanson added desserts (such as brownies and apple cobbler) to a new four-compartment tray. Sadly, Swanson was never able to figure out a way to stuff in a glass of wine or a bottle of beer with the meal.

Shopping for men's office apparel was a cinch in the nineteen fifties, as men's office wear basically consisted of dark blue, brown, and charcoal suits with white or blue shirts and uniform and dark ties. Hats were de rigueur. There was, however, some flexibility in leisurewear; polo shirts, Bermuda shorts, and short-sleeved button-front shirts in bold new designs allowed guys an opportunity to stand out a bit from the crowd. During the fifties pink rage, men also had the option of wearing pink shirts and ties.

Shopping for women's clothing was somewhat more complicated. Females dressed smartly and good grooming and a tailored look were prized. So was an hourglass figure, which was helped by wearing girdles and bras, some of which had more uplift than a Jupiter rocket.

Women wore scarves and gloves. When a woman went swimming she put on a bathing cap and very subdued swimwear—even the skimpiest two-piece suit covered the belly button. When a lady went out at night she slipped on a mink coat if her husband could afford one. Richard Nixon obviously couldn't. In his famous 1952 *Checkers Television Speech* to the American people he said, " . . . Pat doesn't have a mink coat. But she does have a respectable Republican cloth coat."

Unlike today, most stores in the 1950s were shuttered on Sundays. Many states had religion-based "Blue Laws" that compelled such closings. Sunday was a day to rest, go to church, read the papers, watch television, visit friends or relatives, putter about the house, and fantasize about the next car, appliance, or television set that the family was going to buy.

ERASMUS HIGH RECOLLECTIONS

Sometimes called the "mother of high schools," Brooklyn's Erasmus Hall High School started as a small private academy in 1787 with a student body of 26 boys. The first secondary school to be chartered by the Regents of the University of the State of New York, it became the hub out of which developed the huge secondary system of school education in New York. The original academy building, a superb example of colonial architecture with its clapboards and hand-carved beams, sits in the center of an ivy-towered quadrangle. It was constructed in 1787 with funds contributed by Alexander Hamilton, John Jay, Aaron Burr, and others. Surrounding it are three-story stone and brick buildings, Collegiate Gothic in design. In front of the old academy is a large bronze statue of Desiderius Erasmus, copied from an original created in 1622 by Dutch sculptor Hendrick de Keiser.

When I attended Erasmus from 1958-1962 the place had a kind of English prep school atmosphere. My biology teacher wore spats, my Spanish teacher made us stand to do verb conjugations, and my social studies teacher addressed his students by their surnames preceded by Miss or Mister. Our principal, Dr. John F. McNeill (a former US Air Force colonel who wore white shirts with pointed collars, ties, and vests), was a strict headmaster. He demanded total silence at assemblies and if a teacher came in a minute late, Miss Grace L. Corey, Dr. McNeill's administrative assistant, docked them.

Erasmus was one of perhaps half a dozen New York City public schools that offered classical Greek. In music class students were taught Christmas hymns in Latin. Other schools sent their charges to study hall; at Erasmus we went to "chapel"—which was the auditorium with its magnificent stained-glass windows.

Erasmus was the sole high school in Brooklyn sans female cheerleaders, a practice that dated back to the olden days when it was unacceptable for young ladies to show themselves. Student government representatives were required to wear shirts and ties. The Christmas and spring concerts were held at Brooklyn College.

In 1962, the year I graduated, Erasmus students won five National Westinghouse Science scholarships (the most in the country), which brought the school's total to 23 awards in the scholarship's 21-year history. In 1963, Erasmus made the top-ten list of the National Academy of Sciences for sending the most graduates on to PhD programs.

Erasmus has had a number of famous and accomplished attendees, including actress and comedienne Mae West (class of 1893), Pulitzer-prize-winning author Bernard Malamud (1932), mystery writer Mickey Spillane (1936), opera singer Beverly Sills (she attended in the 1940s before transferring), and singer/songwriter Neil Diamond (1954-1956). Barbra Streisand graduated three years before me with a 91 GPA. Chess champion Bobby Fischer didn't bother to graduate. He dropped out of Erasmus in 1961, saying that formal education had little more to offer him. I know how he felt.

Playing stickball and goofing off with my friends were my main interests during my adolescence. I considered going to school and taking part in extracurricular activities as major disruptions, though I did join the audiovisual club in my senior year at Erasmus because I thought having at least one extramural interest on my college applications would look good to university admissions committees. I barely studied for my courses, completed my homework during classes, and intermittently played hooky. Luckily for me, schoolwork came easy and I never had any trouble getting good grades, except for chemistry. (I can't recall why chem gave me so much trouble, but it did and I had to buy a review book and actually read the thing to pass the subject.)

When the weather was good my pals and I occasionally left school early to take trips to Manhattan or Coney Island. One time, when we had cut out of the building, I encountered my father on a bus that was going down Flatbush Avenue. He asked me why I wasn't in school and I told him that I felt sick and needed to go home. When he asked why my friends were with me, I told him they also felt sick and needed to go home. I know he didn't buy my story but he let me slide, saying that he hoped we'd all recover quickly and that he'd call my mother later in the day to find out how I was doing. He never made that call.

My dad had also been a bit of a rebel when he went to school and perhaps the reason that he didn't crack down on his wayward son was because he understood the urge that can come over a guy, when the sun is shining brightly and the breeze is softly blowing, to abandon one's responsibilities and frolic and caper on the streets and avenues of the greatest city in the greatest nation in the world. Maybe when he ran into me on the bus he was experiencing that longing too, and that's why he was traveling through Brooklyn in the middle of the day rather than being at his place of work in the Bronx.

Every now and then, my buddies and I were forced to serve detention for our school misdeeds. To relieve the boredom of incarceration, when the teacher wasn't looking, we would sometimes shoot water at each other from the water pistols that we carried on us. If you were caught shooting a water gun you received double detention and the "waterarm" was confiscated with the proviso that you would get it back if your parent came to school to retrieve it. I lost a couple of water pistols to the school authorities because I thought it prudent not to tell my parents that I was bringing liquid weaponry to school and that I was being made to serve time for academic crime. I also shot cap guns in Erasmus's hallowed halls, something that would probably land a youngster behind bars if he or she did that today.

The students at Erasmus were similar in many ways but there was a divergence between the kids who came from the rich part of Flatbush—those who lived on streets like Argyle Road, Albemarle Road, Rugby Road, and Tennis Court—and the kids like me who lived somewhere else. The rich kids weren't any smarter than the rest of us but they dressed better and hung out in a clique. I hung out in a clique, too. My group dressed down, played stickball, pulled pranks, and was devoid of females.

On Friday nights, lots of Erasmanians would go over to Garfield's ("the cafeteria of refinement"), which was located near the corner of Church and Flatbush Avenues, to socialize and hook up for dates. I wasn't part of that relationship-seeking crowd. When I went to Garfield's it was during the day to have their delicious rice pudding with hot fruit sauce on top. Due to my relatively young age (I was barely 16 when I graduated from Erasmus), and passionate interest in sports, I didn't start fraternizing with members of the opposite sex till I was in college.

I don't remember the names of any of my teachers or anything about my high school graduation. But I do remember throwing pennies into the book that Desi, the Desiderius Erasmus statue, was holding to get good luck before taking New York State Regents exams; forging my mother's signature on notes from my teachers that described less than stellar behavior on my part; and the feeling of dread that was constantly with me in my senior year that life after high school would be bleak and full of unwanted responsibilities. Happily, college proved me wrong on that score.

The 1950s: An Auto-Manic Nation

Pent-up demand and a boom economy led to sweeping developments in the automotive world of the 1950s. Cars became longer, wider, faster, and more glitzy. Extra chrome was added, a sign that America had metal to squander. The fifties also saw some of the best-looking and the weirdest vehicles ever created: e.g., the Ford Thunderbird and Ford Edsel.

The dawn of the "jet age" brought with it many industrial and design improvements in automotive engineering. One major technological advance was the tremendous rapidity with which cars could be made. On the design side, auto stylists capitalized on America's fascination with jet-propelled aircraft by reconfiguring run-of-the-mill family cars into ultramodern chariots with wings, turbines, and after-burner taillights. Drivers of these conveyances could make believe they were pilots and they never had to leave the ground.

Cars in the 1950s had individuality even within the same company. Unlike today, when you can hardly tell one vehicle from another, differences could be discerned among a Buick, Cadillac, Oldsmobile, Pontiac, or Chevrolet without having to hunt for the emblem. A high-roofed Chrysler was not apt to be misidentified as a long flat Ford or a muscular General Motors car.

Performance was a big part of auto marketing. While sporty two-seaters, such as the Corvette, were advertised as being fast, sedans were also pretty quick due to improvements in engine-displacement size and high-octane gas. Young people transformed older vehicles into "hot rods," which were "souped up" for speed and drag raced down remote country roads and tranquil city streets. Besides their emphasis on power and performance, hot rods made a social statement having to do with rebellion, skill, and self-reliance.

Cadillac, a luxury gadget-filled contraption, chock-a-block with chrome and flamboyantly finned, proved that America had come out of the war richer than ever. Cadillac ownership was a symbol of affluence and achievement. It was something to aspire to. Elvis owned a Caddy (actually, Elvis owned a number of Caddies). So did CEOs, Hollywood celebrities and even the man in the street who was able to save enough. President Dwight D. Eisenhower rode in a Cadillac Eldorado during the 1953 Inauguration Day parade. "If you've earned it, why hesitate?" asked Cadillac commercials.

People weren't interested in cheap, compact cars during the fifties. When Henry J. Kaiser and his son Edgar introduced the Henry J motorcar in 1950, an inexpensively priced vehicle with a four-cylinder engine that got 25 miles per gallon, they found that out pretty quickly as sales declined each year the auto was sold. The make was finally discontinued in 1954 (production on a slightly larger six-cylinder model came to a halt in 1955). For the car-driving public, bigger was better, and with gas selling at around 27 cents a gallon few people felt the need to economize.

Dream cars and concept cars helped to capture the public's mood for automotive novelty. The 1951 Buick LeSabre, designed by General Motors' styling guru Harley J. Earl, had an aluminum and magnesium body, heated seats, built-in hydraulic jacks, and a moisture sensor, which raised the top if it started to rain. The 1958 GM Firebird III featured a twin bubble cockpit, ultrasonic key entry, and a joystick controller to accelerate, brake, and steer. GM showed off their dream cars, concept cars, and other fancy prototypes via a Las Vegas-style Motorama show that toured the nation from 1953 to 1961.

"Dynamic obsolescence," a strategy conceived by CEO and GM Board President Alfred P. Sloan to boost demand for new cars, led to annual model changes. While this approach benefited big automakers with deep pockets, it also raised expenditures that hampered the profits of smaller companies. During the 1950s and 1960s ten car firms were whittled down to four. The casualties included Studebaker-Packard, Nash, Hudson, Kaiser-Frazer, Willys, and Crosley.

The following timeline shows some yearly developments in 1950s cars. Think "size," "style," "innovation," and "luxury" as you peruse the various entries. That's what was on the mind of car manufacturers when they were designing and selling their automobiles during the nineteen fifties.

1950s Automobile Timeline

1950: As an option on the 1950 Chevrolet, automatic transmission becomes available in the low-priced field. A new Chevy business coupe costs $1,329. Goodyear offers puncture-sealing tires.

1951: Chrysler marks the beginning of "the Horsepower Race" with the introduction of the 180-horsepower, 331-cubic-inch Firepower Hemi V-8 engine. Kaiser debuts a padded dashboard and pop-out windshield for safety. Chrysler introduces power steering.

1952: Over 2 million cars are sold with automatic transmissions. Packard presents power brakes. Cadillac and Oldsmobile offer Electric Eye headlight dimmers.

1953: Chevrolet unveils the Corvette with its fiberglass body, wraparound windshield, and no side windows. Studebaker promotes sleek, low, restyled models featuring "the European look." Auto air-conditioning becomes available. Motels now outnumber hotels—two to one.

1954: Buick, Oldsmobile, and Cadillac offer wraparound panoramic windshields on all production models. Studebaker merges with Packard; Nash merges with Hudson. GM features several new concept cars at the 1954 GM Motorama, including the 370—horsepower turbine-powered Firebird I and the sporty Nomad station wagon.

1955: The two-seater Ford Thunderbird comes onto the market. Some manufacturers, like Dodge, offer three-tone paint jobs. It's a record sales year, with 7,915,000 cars sold.

1956: Packard premieres power door locks. Chrysler features an in-car record player—the "Hiway Hi-Fi." Over 7,000 drive-in movie theaters dot the nation. Congress approves construction of the 41,000-mile Interstate highway system, the result of which will push more people into the suburbs and decrease passenger rail travel.

1957: Chevy, Pontiac, and Rambler offer fuel injection. Chrysler presents cars with sleek, futuristic styling and monster tailfins;

Plymouth ads boast "Suddenly, it's 1960!" Ford introduces the Edsel, a car nobody wants and very few buy. The average car price is $2749. Two-thirds of all automobiles are purchased on credit.

1958: Chrysler introduces the day-night rearview mirror and cruise control. GM offers air suspension on several models. An economic recession causes car sales to plummet 31%. The federal government mandates retail price stickers on cars. The first Toyotas and Datsuns are imported.

1959: Tailfins reach their zenith with the Cadillac Eldorado, the ultimate Space Age vehicle. Toyota opens its first plant outside Japan—in Brazil—marking the start of their efforts to localize production and design of their cars. Responding to foreign imports eating into domestic auto sales and hard economic times, GM, Ford, and Chrysler introduce "compact cars," specifically the Chevrolet Corvair, Ford Falcon, and Plymouth Valiant. The era of outsized chrome and full-size fins on super-sized auto bodies is over.

STICKBALL REMINISCENCES

During the 1950s, my friends and I were obsessed with playing stickball, a street game related to baseball that was very popular among kids living in big northeastern American cities at the time. Every day after school, as long as it wasn't pouring rain or unbearably cold, we'd get together on our field of dreams, the street in front of my apartment building, to take part in a sport that required minimal equipment (a sawed-off broom handle and a rubber ball) and produced maximal enjoyment. Nothing was more fun or important to me than being actively engaged in a stickball contest.

We played pick-up games, usually two or three guys to a side. There was no pitcher; you hit the ball yourself. Home plate and second base were manhole covers in the middle of the street; first and third were automobiles located on opposite sides of the road. The foul lines were the curbs of the sidewalk, and parked cars were considered fair territory. When a ball was put into play the batter had to run the "bases." The score of the game was kept with chalk marks on the asphalt pavement.

A two-sewer shot (the round sewer covers in the middle of the street were standard measuring units in stickball) was considered a formidable blast. If you smacked a ball past two sewers (pronounced "*soo*-uhs") you were up there with the likes of Duke Snider, Mickey Mantle, and Willie Mays. I never saw or knew anyone who hit a three-sewer shot, which, had it been done, would have been deemed a miracle on my block analogous to parting the waters of the Red Sea or turning Lot's wife into a pillar of salt.

Our games were lively, absorbing, and highly competitive, and hits in the clutch or "exceptional plays," like diving onto the hood or trunk of a parked car to catch a fly ball, were preserved in local folklore. Occasionally, some of the neighborhood girls, sitting on the stoops with their portable transistor radios blaring the latest rock and roll songs and blabbing with each other, would glance around to see what we boys were screaming about. This gave us extra incentive to do well, as it meant we had an audience to perform for.

One of our ground rules was that a batter was not allowed to hit if a car was coming down the street, but most of the time no one paid any attention to that regulation. Screeching car brakes and thunderous horn blasts were part and parcel of our afternoon delights, and so were nervous mothers, who silently prayed that their stickball-playing sons were not being run over and maimed by passing automobiles.

Speaking of mothers, every night at dusk my mom would signal me to come in for dinner by hanging a white handkerchief attached to the end of a broken bow (part of an old toy bow-and-arrow set) out of our fifth-story kitchen window. However, as I was usually concentrating on hitting, fielding, or gabbing with my friends, I frequently ignored her symbolic entreaty. This sometimes spurred my mother to shout from the window, "Your father just got home and he expects you to join the family for dinner without delay. You better come up right away if you know what's good for you." Those words usually got me upstairs immediately, as my dad did not suffer fools or children who came in late for meals gladly.

My mother would often drop money out the window when she wanted me to shop for the family and I was playing in the street. The way she engineered the money drop was to put coins or bills, or at times both, into an envelope that she sealed with scotch tape. She'd then wrap the envelope in a handkerchief, tie the hankie up tightly, and sail the entire parcel down to the sidewalk. If only paper money was involved she would often add a roller skate key to the contents so the packet would not blow around on its downward trip. None of her "money packs" ever broke open on the pavement, even though many of them were heavily laden with change. (Unlike many people who work in the world of high finance, my mother clearly knew how to safely transfer currency.)

On the weekends, my buddies and I would play stickball from early morning to late afternoon, skipping lunch and going to Mom and Pop's candy store, located around the corner from our "athletic field," afterward to have egg creams (iconic Brooklyn beverages made with a little milk, a dash of Fox's U-bet chocolate syrup, and plain seltzer), cherry lime rickeys, malted milk shakes, or cokes. Over our drinks we'd discuss and analyze the games we'd just engaged in and revise our batting averages to reflect our hitting performances in those games.

We always had a great time in the candy store acting silly and telling jokes, often at the expense of Mom or Pop. For example, one day my friend Sandy asked Pop, "Do you have Sir Walter Raleigh (pipe tobacco) in a pouch?" When Pop said he did, Sandy responded, "Well, you better let him out because he's suffocating." Another time, Sandy asked Mom if she knew where the yellow went when she brushed her teeth with Pepsodent. Those were the good stickball days—but there were harrowing stickball days as well.

When I was ten I had a batting slump. No matter how hard I tried I was not able to hit a rubber Spalding ball with a wooden stickball bat. I became an easy out and as a result I was the last person chosen to be on a team. I couldn't concentrate on my schoolwork, I couldn't enjoy TV, and I couldn't eat. I thought myself a totally worthless human being. I longed for the two-sewer shots I had always been able to thump out, the solid line drives that careened off parked cars, and the adulation of my ball-playing buddies. But I just couldn't hit.

One day, as I lay sobbing on my bed thinking about my failed athletic prowess, my mother walked through the door and asked, "What's the matter?" I could barely get the words out through my tears. "I'm in a batting slump. I can't hit. I'm washed up. No one wants me on their side. I wish I was dead."

She gave me a "mother will make it all better" look and then said, "Everyone has slumps. Your father has times when he's not very effective at the office. I have weeks when it's tough for me to accomplish what I want to do. Even God isn't perfect. The trick is to keep on going and not get down on yourself."

Her supportive words boosted my sagging spirits, but her offer to pitch sock balls to me across the living room floor saved my life. For one week, in the late afternoon before my father came home from work, my mother threw rolled up balls of socks to me in the living room, which I tried to hit with my stickball bat. To my surprise, I was able to smash those sock balls with complete authority. Lamps fell, the aerial was knocked off the TV, and knick-knacks went flying every which way, as my batted sock balls found their marks. My mother said nothing about the damage I was causing. Instead, after each successful whack, she shouted, "good hit" or "excellent shot." My self-confidence soared. By the following the week I was once again slamming two-sewer blasts and my stickball chums were picking me first in the choose-up games on our block.

Some adults have fond memories of the toys their parents gave them or the trips they took them on. I barely remember those things. My fondest childhood memory is my 5'2" mother, who knew next to nothing about sports, pitching easy to hit sock balls and encouraging words to a distraught, stressed-out kid in a cramped, pre-war Brooklyn apartment house.

My stickball days ended in 1962 when my friends and I graduated from high school and went off to various colleges. Although I've learned quite a lot in school over the years, stickball taught me many useful life skills, such as how to be a good team player, the value of hustle, the importance of grace under pressure, and how to handle victory and defeat. And my stickball-coach-mother taught me that hard work and practice can keep you going when all looks bleak and get you back into the game.

THE 1950s: POPULAR FADS

There were lots of fads in the 1950s. Many of them were spread by television, a technology that achieved prominence during the decade. Some of the fads stuck and are still with us today. The following list contains a number of the more popular fifties fads.

Hula Hoops

Inspired by an Australian calisthenics exercise that involved twirling a three-foot bamboo ring, Arthur Melin and Richard Knerr, owners and co-founders of Wham-O Manufacturing, introduced a plastic version to America in 1957 that they labeled the *hula hoop*. Soon people everywhere were whirling hula hoops round their hips. Roughly 100 million hula hoops were sold worldwide in 1958 and not all by Wham-O, as the company had problems patenting the simple polyethylene plaything.

The Russians criticized the hula hoop as embodying the "emptiness of American culture" and Japan banned it completely. But in most other places and in America especially, lots of folks got a kick out of "hula hooping," more dexterous hoopers swung hula hoops on their arms and legs or about their necks; some spun more than one hoop at a time. By the end of 1958, the hula-hoop craze had petered out. But Richard Knerr found another fascinating and fun gizmo to take its place: the Frisbee.

Frisbees

In 1957, Richard Knerr decided to boost sales at Wham-O by giving the "Pluto Platter" plastic discs he was selling the added brand name "Frisbee" after hearing that East Coast college students were labeling the Pluto Platter with that moniker. The tag caught on and sales took off due to Wham-O's clever marketing of Frisbee playing as a new sport. Although overshadowed by the hula hoop in the 1950s, the Frisbee has remained popular through six decades, with over 200 million units sold. (The name Frisbee derives from the Bridgeport, Connecticut-based Frisbie Baking Company, whose empty pie tins were tossed around for fun by collegians.)

Davy Crockett Coonskin Caps

As a result of five televised Walt Disney *Frontierland* installments, aired during 1954 and 1955, Tennessee frontiersman Davy Crockett went from being a 19th-century historical footnote to a folk hero and an American trendsetter who generated a must-have article of clothing: the coonskin cap with a raccoon tail. During the fifties, kids bought these caps like there was no tomorrow. At the height of the fad in the summer of 1955, coonskin caps sold upward of 5,000 a day, which led to a shortage of coonskins and their replacement by muskrat, rabbit, and fox skins to produce the headwear.

Most fads that come in with a rush go out just as fast. And so it was with Davy Crockett and his coonskin cap. The "King of the Wild Frontier" didn't even get a TV series of his own.

Slinkies

The *Slinky*, a helical spring that can travel down stairs end-over-end as it stretches and re-forms itself, was an accidental byproduct of World War II research concerned with developing coils to support sensitive equipment on ships. It was first introduced to the public in 1945 at a Gimbels department store in Philadelphia. Sales rose quickly and soared in the 1950s when Slinkies were advertised on television—100 million Slinkies were sold in the first 10 years. In 1952, the Slinky Dog debuted. Other Slinky variations marketed in the 1950s include the Slinky train Loco, the Slinky worm Suzie, and the Slinky Crazy Eyes.

Mr. Potato Head

Mr. Potato Head, a plastic model of a potato that can be decorated with a variety of attachable plastic parts such as eyes and ears to make a face, was invented and developed by George Lerner, a Brooklyn-born toy inventor, in 1949 and subsequently manufactured and distributed by Hasbro in 1952. In 1953, Mrs. Potato Head was added. Soon thereafter, Brother Spud and Sister Yam joined the Potato Head family, along with a line of accessories reflecting the prosperity of the fifties. That included a car, a boat trailer, a kitchen set, a stroller, and pets called Spud-ettes. Mr. Potato Head was the first toy advertised on television, the fruits of which helped Hasbro sell over one million kits in its first year.

Scrabble

In 1952, Jack Strauss, the president of Macy's, played and enjoyed Scrabble on a holiday. Upon returning to work Strauss was surprised to learn that the word game was not on sale at his famous New York department store. Once there, the games flew off the shelves and playing Scrabble became a nationwide phenomenon. Within two years, Selchow & Righter, Scrabble's manufacturer, sold over four million sets. Since then, over 150 million Scrabble games have been bought worldwide and Scrabble sets are found in one out of every three American homes.

Jukeboxes

In the 1950s, teenagers hung around ice cream parlors, diners, drug stores, and other places that had jukeboxes to socialize, drink cokes, maybe dance a little, and listen to the new sounds of rock and roll. Operating a jukebox was easy. You dropped in a nickel, selected a song, and voilà—music from a 45-rpm vinyl record.

Jukeboxes were color-blind at a segregated time in America and they allowed whites an opportunity to accept and listen to black performers.

They also gave kids a chance to hear white recording artists play music that their parents might not have approved of. Jukebox popularity declined after the mid-1960s but today there are retro-themed stores and restaurants, like the Johnny Rockets chain, that still have jukeboxes in their establishments.

Chrome and Fins on Cars

The chrome and tailfin era of automobile styling occurred during the 1950s and 1960s, peaking between 1958 and 1960. It was a fashion that took on global proportions, as foreign car designers imitated styling trends from the American auto industry. The 1959 Cadillac Eldorado had tailfins that towered three and a half feet above the pavement and terminated in multiple taillights. They were the largest and most outrageous fins ever put on a regular production car. But those rear-end adornments proved to be too much for lots of customers and tailfins shrank after that point. Vestigial tailfins remained on American cars into the 1980s, with the sides of the quarter panels often being raised above the trunk lid and the corner sharp-edged, or at least lifted.

The Pink Rage

The color pink was ubiquitous in the 1950s, even showing up in men's wear. Tough guys wore pink ties, shirts, and bathrobes and staid businessmen donned pink under their gray flannel suits. There were pink bathrooms with matching accessories, pink cosmetics, pink poodles, pink appliances, pink dishes, and pink telephones; rock and roll singles that celebrated the joys of acquiring "Pink Pedal Pushers" (1958), "Pink Shoe Laces" (1959), and a "White Sport Coat [with a Pink Carnation]" (1957); the musical number "Think Pink!" in the movie *Funny Face*, and Elvis' pink Cadillac. (While no carmaker offered pink as a standard color, the attention the public gave to Elvis' Caddy led many individual car owners in the 1950s to paint their cars various shades of pink.) Pink was also a standard color of women's undergarments, which led Richard Nixon to use this Red-baiting line against Helen Gahagan Douglas in his 1950 Senate campaign: "She's pink right down to her underwear!"

College Fads

College students, a group constantly inventing or propagating new fads, latched on to quite a few during the 1950s. One such whim was *panty raids*, which were normally engaged in with equal zest by the raiders and the raided. Although the raids occasionally got out of control and turned into crazy mayhem, for the most part they were harmless fun. Collegians also engaged in *phone booth stuffing*, which involved cramming as many people as possible into a telephone booth, and *hunkering*, a popular campus fad in which students squatted on their haunches to study or when interacting with each other. In 1959, *Time* noted that hunkerers were urging steel-strike negotiators to hunker awhile and advising Eisenhower and Khrushchev that hunkering would give them a better chance to hammer out agreements at the summit.

Some Other Fifties Fads

TV Dinners	Wiffle ball	TV trays
Drive-in theaters	Bubble gum cigars	Crew cuts
Letter sweaters	Saddle shoes	Legos
Abstract expressionism	Searching for flying saucers	Ant farms
Diners	Pompadour hairdos	Sideburns
Teenyboppers	Beanies (caps)	Beehive hair
DA haircuts	Blue jeans	Cinch belts
Blue suede loafers	Poodle skirts	Fast food
Sock hops	Pez	Gumby
Paint-by-number	Tupperware	Tiki culture
Flattops	Hopalong Cassidy guns	Neon signs
Creepers (shoes)	Bazooka Joe	3-D movies
Carhops	Silly Putty	Disneyland
Chlorophyll	Model making	Erector sets

A Club Med for Kids on the Streets of Brooklyn

Growing up in my Brooklyn neighborhood in the 1950s was like being at a Club Med for kids—so many enjoyable activities to engage in each day, and because I had a stay-at-home mom who cooked, meals were part of the package.

Punchball, a game similar to baseball that involves hitting a soft pink rubber ball—typically a "Spaldeen"—with a closed fist to put it into play, was one of my favorite pursuits. When I attended elementary and junior high school I played punchball every day at lunchtime in the schoolyard. After school, I played punchball in the street in front of my apartment building. I was preternaturally punch drunk for punchball.

Because you could adapt the rules to narrow the field and include "pegging" (throwing the ball at an advancing runner for an out) and "homing" (throwing the ball towards home plate, even though no catcher was being used), you could play punchball with as few as two players to a team. That was a big advantage if only a few guys showed up to participate. But what if only one guy showed up? No problem. You could play *stoopball.*

Stoopball, which entailed throwing a Spaldeen against the front stairs of the semi attached houses where my friends Sandy Litwin and Jonny Ross lived, was a very popular pastime for the ball-playing crowd in my Brooklyn nabe. Although Sandy's and Jonny's mothers weren't especially happy to have balls banging off the steps to the entrance of their houses, they usually didn't chase us away. Their fathers, alas, were not as understanding, and if we didn't want to be subjected to long and boring lectures on the sanctity of private property and the importance of respecting the wishes of your elders, we had to have our games come to a halt before Mr. Litwin or Mr. Ross came home from work.

The rules of stoopball were simple. You threw the ball against the stairs and tried to catch it on a fly or on a bounce—if you caught it on a bounce you got five points, on a fly you got ten. A "pointer" was a ball that hit the edge of a step and came back as a hard line drive that could "knock your teeth out." Catching a pointer on the fly was worth 100 points. Usually the winning score was 1,000 points, but it could be anything agreed upon. If you dropped the ball at any time you were out and your opponent took over. You were also out if you threw the ball and missed the steps entirely, a bonehead play that earned you the wrath of Mrs. Litwin or Mrs. Ross, as those two ladies didn't like Spaldeens slamming into their front doors.

Lots of famous people have played stoopball. Sandy Koufax began his Hall of Fame baseball career by playing the game, while sports announcer Marv Albert missed stoopball so much that he once had a stoop constructed at his house in the suburbs. Billy Joel played stoopball growing up in Hicksville, Long Island. Makes me like him more than I already do.

I also played *boxball*, a delightful diversion that requires just two sidewalk squares (or "boxes" as they were known in street lingo) and a red rubber ball and can be thought of as a postage-size game of tennis sans rackets.

In boxball a player serves, volleys, and defends his square. The ball is slapped back and forth between the boxes with an open palm. The lines (or "cracks") around the concrete define the court; the seam between the two squares is the imaginary net. Slap the ball into your opponent's box; he slaps it back to your box after one bounce or on the fly. You lose the volley if you fail to return a shot, if your return shot's first bounce lands out of your opponent's box, or if you step into the playing court (doing that was my Achilles heel though it was usually my forefoot that caused the foul). Winner of the volley maintains serve and only the server can win a point. Twenty-one is the winning score and you have to win by two points.

There's quite a bit of athleticism to boxball. For example, you can try to hit the ball with force or with a cutting motion to give the ball more spin, which is known as putting on "English," and makes it harder to return. The "reverse shot," using the back of the palm to hit the ball, is a particularly difficult maneuver to execute properly as the back of the palm is not as flat or flexible as the front. Whenever I hit a good reverse shot, the memory of it lingered fondly in my mind for a long time afterwards.

In the winter, I played two-hand *touch football* in the street. It was a sport where the quarterback might tell you to "Cut in front of the '57 parked Chevy" or "Zigzag after you get to the manhole cover." Guys sometimes argued over whether they'd been touched by one hand or two. We once decided to go to Prospect Park and play tackle football to see what that would be like. Luckily no one broke anything but at the end of the day, and for some days afterwards, there was lots of pain and suffering. After that experience, we all resolved that we valued our lives too much to continue to play tackle football and that we'd stick to touch despite the occasional squabble.

Striking a penny placed on the crack between two sidewalk squares with a red rubber ball was the object of *Hit the Penny*, an activity that took place on the same "athletic grounds" as boxball. If you hit the penny you got a point and if the penny flipped over, which was the equivalent of belting a home run in baseball or scoring a touchdown in football, you received two points. Whoever made it to 21 points first won the game. Then it was time for another and still another match until it became dark and you had to go up to dinner.

Sometimes I played *Johnny-on-the-pony*, a game where three or four guys would line up with their heads against each other's rear ends, and other guys would take flying leaps, trying to get as far as they could over the line of backs. Miraculously, no one ever got hurt. It typically ended up with a pile of kids on the ground and a bunch of sore backs for a day or two. I also took part in stickball and roller hockey contests in the street, and flipped baseball cards and pitched pennies off the apartment-building walls on my block for fun.

When lousy weather prevented me from recreating outside, I'd invite my friends to come over to my house or I'd go over to theirs to partake in board games like *Clue* (a deduction game that involves suspects, weapons and rooms); *Chinese Checkers* (a game where the objective is to place one's pieces in the corner opposite one's starting position of a pitted hexagram by single moves or jumps over other pieces); or, my number one all-time favorite board game, *Ethan Allen's All Star Baseball* (a game involving two spinners atop a diagram of a baseball field and circular cards divided into sections that simulate individual player statistics). My buddies and I could spend hours playing board games and when we finished we'd just shoot the breeze. Or, if the climate improved, we'd go outside and play some sort of ball game.

There was always something doing in my neighborhood. No need to make play dates. The term didn't even exist. You simply went outdoors, or stayed inside during rotten weather, and the games began. As a kid you couldn't have asked for a better resort to live in. And the accommodations were free.

The 1950s: Four Iconic Superstars

𝔈lvis 𝔓resley

Elvis Presley began his career in 1954 as a performer of rockabilly music, an up-tempo blend of R&B and country with a strong backbeat. After hitting it big in 1956, he became the leading figure of the new sound of rock and roll. A 20th-century American icon widely known by a single name, Elvis is often referred to as *The King of Rock and Roll* or, simply, *The King*.

In 1955, after releasing five songs with the Memphis-based Sun Record Company and gaining some measure of fame in the South, Elvis hired "Colonel" Tom Parker, a former carnival barker who promoted dancing chickens, to be his personal manager. The colonel hit the ground running, quickly shifting his client over to RCA Records, a major national recording corporation. Parker also quickly launched a massive promotional campaign aimed at getting Elvis national exposure.

Elvis first appeared on CBS's *The Dorsey Brothers Stage Show*. On *The Steve Allen Show*, he sang *Hound Dog* to a live basset hound dressed in a tuxedo. His hip gyrations on Milton Berle's *Texaco Star Theater* earned him the nickname *Elvis the Pelvis*—which concerned Ed Sullivan, who booked Elvis anyway for three performances on the family-friendly *Ed Sullivan Show*. By the third performance, Ed was "cropping" Presley—displaying the singer only from the waist up (which didn't fool anyone, since everybody knew what was going on from the waist down). Approximately 60 million people, the largest single audience in history to that date, saw Elvis sing *Don't Be Cruel* on that show.

In January 1956, Elvis recorded 11 songs for RCA. Among them was *Heartbreak Hotel*, which became Elvis' first Number 1 hit. Elvis tore up the charts for the rest of the decade, despite the fact that from 1958 to 1959 he was serving in the army. Elvis also acted in movies during the fifties, with starring roles in *Love Me Tender* (1956), *Jailhouse Rock* (1957), and *King Creole* (1958).

Elvis and his music captivated teenagers all across America during the 1950s and they flocked to his concerts in droves. But many of their parents were not as enamored. They viewed Elvis as a symbol of teen rebellion and for some, "anti-Negro" prejudice toward rock and roll (many rock singers were black) increased their dislike. But negative vibes from their moms and dads didn't bother his young fans. If anything, it made Elvis more popular with them. Eight of The King's lifetime Top Ten songs are from the 1950s.

Marlon Brando

Marlon Brando, whom many consider the greatest movie actor who ever lived, wowed the public in 1951 with his performance as Stanley Kowalski in Elia Kazan's screen adaptation of Tennessee Williams's *A Streetcar Named Desire*. He was nominated for an Academy Award for that role and for the leading parts that he played over the next three years in *Viva Zapata!* (1952*), Julius Caesar* (1953), and *On the Waterfront* (1954). The "I coulda been a contenda" scene in that last film is one of the most famous scenes in motion picture history and the line itself has become part of America's cultural lexicon.

In 1953, Brando starred in *The Wild One* riding his own Triumph Thunderbird motorcycle 6T, which dismayed Triumph dealers, as the movie's subject matter concerned biker gangs taking over a small town. They needn't have worried. The images of Brando posing with his Triumph motorcycle and wearing short sideburns, a Perfecto motorcycle jacket, and tilted cap became trendy, greatly boosting sales of black leather motorcycle jackets, Triumph motorcycles, jeans, white caps, and sunglasses. Brando's hairstyle also stimulated a craze for sideburns that was imitated by James Dean, Elvis Presley, and lots of other guys.

Kids who watched *The Wild One* identified with Brando's character, insurgent gang leader Johnny Stabler who responds to a townie who asks him "What are you rebelling against?" with the bravado-filled rejoinder "Whaddya got?" Parents were not too happy with that come back or with the influence that Brando and *The Wild One* were having on their progeny. But movie director Nicholas Ray liked what he saw. Inspired by the gang image from *The Wild One,* Ray lifted it for *Rebel Without a Cause,* further demonstrating Brando's allure for young people.

Brando played a number of roles in the 1950s that went beyond just being a tough guy: singing gambler Sky Masterson in *Guys and Dolls*; Sakini, a Japanese interpreter for the US Army in *The Teahouse of the August Moon*; an Air Corps flier with a southern accent in *Sayonara;* and a Nazi officer in *The Young Lions.* Though he received an Oscar nomination for his acting in *Sayonara,* by the close of the 1950s Brando's performing had lost much of its energy and focus.

James Dean

James Dean has become a cultural icon in large part because of his featured role as Jim Stark, a troubled LA teenager, in the movie *Rebel Without a Cause* (1955). Two other roles that support his icon status are the loner Cal Trask in *East of Eden* (1955) and the truculent Texas farmer Jett Rink in *Giant* (1956). Dean's continuing fame and popularity is based on these three films, the only ones he starred in before his untimely demise in a car crash at the age of 24. His death at an early age has strengthened his legendary status.

Teens in the fifties connected with Dean and the parts he played in his movies, especially the rebel-without-a-cause outsider Jim Stark, an angst-ridden, mixed-up, 17-year-old kid whom no one, not even his peers, can get a handle on. Jimbo's archetypal scream to his bickering parents—"You're tearing me apart!"—had particular resonance for adolescent viewers of *Rebel Without a Cause,* a film that saw the debut of teen actors Natalie Wood, Sal Mineo, and Dennis Hopper.

Both men and women found Dean appealing, like fellow motion picture stars Rock Hudson and Montgomery Clift. His concern for the lovesick gay character Plato in *Rebel Without a Cause* impressed gays for its truthfulness. Girls found everything Dean said and did in *Rebel* super sexy. Straight guys related to Dean's brooding Angry Young Man persona.

At the 1955 Academy Awards, Dean received a posthumous Best Actor in a Leading Role nomination for his role as Cal Trask in *East of Eden*, the first official posthumous acting nomination in Academy Awards history. At the 1956 Academy Awards, he received his second posthumous Best Actor Academy Award nomination for his role in *Giant*. Dean is the only person to ever have received two such acting nominations. A year after he passed away, as many as 8,000 fans a month were writing to the dead James Dean, more than were writing to any living actor.

Marilyn Monroe

Marilyn Monroe, a woman who embodied the twin desires for sexuality and innocence in American society, was the ultimate movie sex goddess of the 1950s. Her apparent vulnerability and purity, mixed with an inborn sensuality, endeared her to the world. Some have called Monroe the most famous woman of the 20th century.

Monroe's early roles were minor, but her performances in *The Asphalt Jungle* and *All About Eve* (both 1950) were well received. It was her acting in *Niagara* (1953), however, that propelled her to stardom. Monroe played Rose Loomis, a beautiful young wife who plots to kill her older, jealous husband (Joseph Cotten). Monroe's success in *Niagara* was followed with lead parts in the immensely popular *Gentlemen Prefer Blondes* and *How to Marry a Millionaire*.

In March 1952, Monroe faced a potential scandal when a nude photo of her, taken by a photographer three years earlier, surfaced at a film studio she was working for. To head off trouble, Monroe suggested to the studio execs that she should simply admit she had posed for the photograph but emphasize she had done so only because she needed money to pay her rent. Her subsequent interview saying that produced lots of public sympathy for her plight as a struggling actress trying to get by.

In 1953, *Photoplay* magazine voted Monroe the Best New Actress of the year and *Playboy* chose her to be their first centerfold. The picture *Playboy* used for that centerfold was purchased from the photographer who did Monroe's 1949 nude-photo shoot.

On January 14, 1954, Monroe married baseball superstar Joe DiMaggio at San Francisco's City Hall. Sadly, her fame and sexual image became a problem that doomed their marriage. Nine months after they wed, Marilyn and Joe divorced.

In 1955, Monroe took a hiatus from Hollywood and moved to New York City to study under Lee Strasberg at the Actor's Studio. The following year she started her own production company and married the playwright Arthur Miller. Friends reported she made him "giddy." The marriage didn't work out and six years later, in 1962, Marilyn was dead (her death was ruled a probable suicide). It was a tragic ending for a highly venerated Hollywood luminary; an actress who once said, "Well-behaved women rarely make history."

Working It Out in Gym

My favorite subjects in high school were history and English. My least preferred subject was gym, a course that I found physically painful and a huge waste of time, as I kept myself in tiptop shape by running around for hours playing all sorts of ball games in the street after school.

My phys ed. teacher was a fat, ruddy-faced fellow with a mean disposition and a hatred for children. Standing on an upturned metal waste paper basket in front of the room, with an evil grin planted on his malevolent puss, he'd sullenly read off the attendance roll. Then he'd stroll around the gym, pushing down firmly on your behind if it was sticking up in the air when you were doing push-ups, and holding your feet to the floor in a vise-like grip to make sure you were doing your sit-ups properly. He never personally demonstrated the correct way to do any of the calisthenics he wanted us to perform because he was so out of shape there was no way he could have done that. And that was lucky for him because the hard-wood gymnasium floor made doing those exercises a literal pain in the ass for all who attempted them, which was definitely not yours truly when the teacher wasn't looking my way.

A particularly horrific form of physical torture we were obliged to carry out was to climb the long thick hemp ropes that hung from the gym's ceiling. Here's how the exercise was done. You put the rope between your legs, out around your knee/calf and back between the insteps of your sneakers. With the rope like this, clamping your feet together acts like a brake and ideally you should be able to brace yourself in that position without using your hands and arms. However, as my classmates and I were not Olympic athletes or army rangers who had just completed basic training, but rather high school students in average condition, most of us had to use our hands and arms to support ourselves. The result was hand and arm strains going up the rope and "Indian rope burns" coming down it.

Worse than performing the ridiculous exercises we were forced to do in class was the reality that when we finished working out, we had to change from our sweaty gym uniforms to street clothes without being able to shower in between. This meant we were unfit for mixed company or indeed any sort of company for the rest of the day. Of course, on the plus side, changing clothes did reduce the amount of time we had to spend actually exercising.

In my junior year, I bought a pair of yellow high-top canvas sneakers to wear in gym. My fellow classmates sported black, white, or blue sneaks and I must say I got a real kick out of being the only guy who had yellow sneakers. They made me feel kind of special and when I looked down at them I was sometimes able to take my mind off the revolting fact that physical education was a required subject that I needed to pass to be able to graduate. I just loved my yellow sneakers. And I wasn't the only one who had fond feelings for my footwear.

One day during gym, Beecher Miller, a tough kid from the projects who had more than a fleeting familiarity with knives, brass knuckles, zip guns, and other "WIDs" (weapons of individual destruction), walked up to me and accused me of stealing *his* yellow sneakers. He said if I didn't give him *his* yellow sneakers that he and his friends would kick my ass and fuck me up after school. These seemed to me to be two very good and compelling reasons for surrendering my colorful athletic shoes, and that is what I did.

When I came home I told my mother about the ruckus that had transpired over my sporting apparel and asked her if she would give me money to buy another pair of yellow sneakers. To my sad surprise and deep disappointment she nixed the request. She said instead that she would be going down to the school to talk to the dean about getting my sneakers back.

I explained to my dear mama that if she contacted the dean then Beecher and his buddies would beat me up or perhaps do much worse things to me, and I begged her to reconsider her decision in the matter. She replied that she was sure the school authorities wouldn't let any harm befall me and that standing up to bullies was the best way to deal with them. I thought a laissez-faire approach, especially when one's life was on the line, was a far better idea and did my best to convince my mater of the merits of that position. But she would not be swayed from seeing the dean.

The following day I was called to the dean's office and, with my mother sitting across from me, I told the dean my tale of woe. When I finished the story he summoned Beecher to his office and directed him to give me back my yellow sneakers and not to injure me in any way. He said if Beecher did this, the incident would be closed but if he didn't, he would be expelled from school and the police would be notified of his transgression. Beecher stared balefully at me the entire time he was in the room but he acquiesced to the dean's conditions. The next day he gave me back my yellow sneakers, which I never wore again to gym.

For the rest of the semester Beecher and his buddies threw me dirty looks in PE class, in the school halls, and in the streets, but they never touched me or said anything nasty to me, which I found astonishing. I thought for sure that Beecher and his cronies would pound me into the pavement and make my existence a living hell, but for reasons that are still unfathomable to me I was spared those dreadful outcomes. However, to be on the safe side, I made it a practice that year to cut out of gym class every once in a while. I figured, no sense tempting fate. And besides, strolling down the boardwalk, driving bumper cars, and playing Skee-ball at Coney Island was a great way to stay fit.

The 1950s: Books and Movies

Books

Home life was of enormous interest to Americans in the 1950s so it's no surprise that *Betty Crocker's Picture Cook Book* and *Better Homes and Gardens Book* made it to the pinnacle of the decade's bestselling book lists. Americans were quite taken with religion, too; *The Secret of Happiness* by Reverend Billy Graham and *The Holy Bible: Revised Standard Edition* were likewise number one bestsellers. And sex and status intrigued the populace; ergo the commercial success of Alfred Kinsey's research report *Sexual Behavior in the Human Female* and Vance Packard's business critique *The Hidden Persuaders*.

Lots of top-selling fictional books published in the fifties also explored the subjects of sex, status, and religion. The following three volumes are notable examples of such texts.

Henry Morton Robinson's 1950 chartbuster *The Cardinal* tells the story of a young Irish-American priest who ascends the ranks of the Catholic Church by learning humility and a commitment to creed as a result of his personal struggles. The book underscores the idea that faith and virtue, if diligently pursued, will triumph in the end. Its tremendous popularity confirmed the importance of religion in America and the idea that there is far more to life than just having a successful career.

The Man in the Gray Flannel Suit, Sloan Wilson's 1955 bestselling novel about man's search for purpose in a world dominated by materialism and corporate ladder climbing, captured the mood of a generation. In 1956, *The Man in the Gray Flannel Suit* was turned into a film featuring Gregory Peck and Jennifer Jones, and both book and movie became very popular. Even Ed Norton, Ralph Kramden's sidekick on *The Honeymooners,* was aware of Wilson's work. On one episode of the show he told Ralph as he emerged from a manhole in full sewer worker regalia, "Who did you expect, the man in the gray flannel suit?"

Peyton Place, a 1956 work of fiction by Grace Metalious, tracks the lives of three women and how they deal with their identity as women and sexual beings in a small New England town. It became a humongous hit, selling 60,000 copies within the first 10 days of its release and remaining on the *New York Times* bestseller list for 59 weeks. In 1957, the book was made into a movie starring Arthur Kennedy and Lana Turner. Later on it provided inspiration for a trendy prime-time TV series that aired from September 1964 until June 1969. Today the term "Peyton Place" has become a cliché to describe a setting where everyone knows everyone else's business.

Among other popular 1950s works of fiction, the next three stand out as important literary narratives that had strong and sometimes long-lasting effects on their readers.

The Catcher in the Rye (1951) by J. D. Salinger, a book named by the Modern Library as one of the 100 best English-language novels of the 20th century, tackles the complex teenage issues of identity, belonging, and connection. The novel, now a staple of the high school curriculum and library registers of banned books, is controversial for its use of coarse language and the undermining of conventional morality. Its protagonist and antihero, Holden Caulfield, a sixteen-year-old preppy-rebel with a cause, has given voice to generations of teens caught between adolescence and the adult world.

Invisible Man, a classic from the moment it first surfaced in 1952, records the trials and tribulations of its narrator—a young, nameless black man—as he encounters intolerance and cultural ignorance in American society. As the title suggests, the main character is invisible because people see him as a stereotype, not as a real person. The book gained its author, Ralph Ellison, the National Book Award for fiction in 1953.

On the Beach, a 1957 bestselling novel by Nevil Shute, deals with world destruction by nuclear weapons and nuclear fallout. Set in 1963, approximately a year after World War III, the book's post-apocalyptic end-of-the-planet theme resonated with a public that was terrified by the possibilities of atomic war between the US and the USSR. *On the Beach* was serialized by many newspapers of the time and adapted for the screenplay of a 1959 movie that was made in the face of opposition from the Pentagon. The film featured Gregory Peck, Ava Gardner, and the legendary hoofer Fred Astaire, who received rave reviews for his superb acting and never danced a step.

Movies

TV came in like gangbusters in the late 1940s and early 1950s, causing movie studios and motion picture companies to look for new ways to get audiences back into theaters. This prompted them to develop widescreen video approaches such as CinemaScope and VistaVision, enhanced sound techniques, and, for a few years, gimmickry like 3-D. Spectacle films compatible with these technologies gained great popularity, with epics like *Quo Vadis* (1951), *The Robe* (1953), *The Ten Commandments* (1956), and *Ben-Hur* (1959).

An increased interest in science due to the A-bomb, Cold War worries, and an intensified curiosity about extraterrestrial life led to the making of lots of science fiction movies in the 1950s. The genre had its golden age in the decade with such noteworthy flicks as *Creature from the Black Lagoon* (originally released in 3-D), *The Day the Earth Stood Still* (which features a fifties icon—a flying saucer), *Them* (a black and white movie about man's encounter with a nest of radiation-giganticized ants), and *Forbidden Planet* (a film that contains a plot similar to Shakespeare's *The Tempest*). There was also terra-firma-based subject matter, featured in motion pictures like *When Worlds Collide* and *20,000 Leagues Under the Sea*.

Over five hundred westerns, including iconic films such as *The Searchers*, *The Far Country*, *Shane*, and *High Noon*, were shot in the 1950s. Celebrating the triumph of the "good guys" over the "bad guys" and the values of honor and sacrifice in stories that were typically set in the American Old West, fifties westerns lifted people's spirits and provided heroes to look up to. Westerns made subsequent to the 1950s were typically not as upbeat, lauding rude and defiant antiheroes and stressing cynicism, violence, and inequality as major themes.

Alfred Hitchcock, a man who directed over 50 feature films in a career spanning more than six decades, was at the top of his form in the 1950s with suspense thrillers like *Stage Fright* (1950), *Strangers on a Train* (1951), *I Confess* (1953), *Dial M for Murder* (1954), *Rear Window* (1954), *To Catch a Thief* (1955), *The Trouble with Harry* (1955), *The Man Who Knew Too Much* (1956), *The Wrong Man* (1956), *Vertigo* (1958), and *North by Northwest* (1959). In 1956, "Hitch" became an American citizen and left England to make the United States his new home. Amazingly, the man who is considered the greatest British movie director of all time received five Academy Award nominations in his lengthy career for directing but never won an Academy Award in that category.

Hollywood made scores of films featuring juvenile delinquency during the 1950s. Among the better ones are *Blackboard Jungle* (1953), *The Wild One* (1953), and *Rebel Without a Cause* (1955). B-movies that exploited the terrors of teen transgression include *Rock All Night* (1957), *High School Confidential* (1958) and *The Bloody Brood* (1959). Young people enjoyed watching all the wrongdoing that was being shown on the silver screen. Their parents worried that the kids would emulate that bad behavior and become criminals. (A number of youths did break the law. The New York *Daily News* reported in 1954 that "rowdyism, riot, and revolt" was the new three *Rs* in New York public schools.)

The 1950s were the most stunning and somber years for Hollywood musicals. On the plus side, two musical films, *An American in Paris* (1951) and *Gigi* (1958), won Academy Awards for Best Motion Picture. However, television drew millions of people away from movie theaters and sped the demise of the studios that had made musical film extravaganzas possible. How great was TV's impact on the cinema? In the mid-1940s, 90 million Americans went to the movies each week—by the late 1950s, that figure had declined to 16 million.

As for dramatic films, the fifties foreshadowed a trend away from motion pictures devised with big studio control to films that featured characters whose conflicts were more inward than outward and actors who brought greater emotional sensitivity and innovative interpretations to their roles. Such movies include motion picture classics like *On the*

Waterfront, *Rebel Without a Cause*, *Marty*, *Paths of Glory*, and *12 Angry Men*. In the 1960s, the studio system continued to decline. The rise of independent producers and directors and new ideas about the depiction of the real world in film is just one more example of how occurrences in the fifties (e.g., the Kinsey Reports, the birth of rock and roll, the beat movement) influenced events in the sixties.

A Brooklyn Woodland Tale

I was 11 years old in 1957, and getting lost in the woods at Prospect Park (a 585-acre urban oasis located in the heart of Brooklyn containing the borough's only forest), with my friend Alan J. Weberman was something I really looked forward to doing on the weekends. The challenge for us was to find our way out of the "wilderness" once we were off the trails and deep into the brush. When that was done it was on to the neighborhood candy store. There, over vanilla egg creams, chocolate Clark bars, Drake's pound cakes, and long salted pretzels taken from a plastic see-through pretzel bin on the counter, we'd discuss how smart and lucky we were to have made it out alive and in one piece from the wilds of Prospect Park.

Unlike the famous 19th-century explorers David Stanley and Robert Livingstone, who had to travel thousands of miles from England to Africa to get to their jungle adventures, all Alan and I had to do was to saunter two and a half blocks from the apartment building where we both lived to get to ours. Once we reached the entrance to Prospect Park it was but a stone's throw to the forest. We took no food or water with us. If we couldn't find our way back to civilization we'd live off the land.

My fellow explorer was a bit of an oddball. Unlike the other guys on the block, Alan, who was a year older than me, wasn't into sports or girls. He was a *beatnik*, a follower of the countercultural and anti-materialist writer Jack Kerouac who introduced the phrase "Beat Generation" into the English language. Like other beats, Alan rejected conformity and embraced a philosophy of "do your own thing" that in his case, and that of his fellow rebels, involved wearing dark sunglasses, berets, black turtleneck sweaters, and playing the bongo drums, the racket of which was a constant irritant to his parents and the neighbors living nearby his apartment.

I thought Alan was real cool. The rest of my friends thought he was nuts. They may have had a point. As an adult, Alan gained minor celebrity by being assaulted by folk singer Bob Dylan because Dylan was angry that Alan kept rummaging through the garbage that Dylan was leaving out for collection. In the guise of AJ Weberman, Alan also popularized the terms "garbology" and "Dylanology"; maintained a 30-year involvement with the Yippies, a counterculture group of the 1960s; and became an activist in the Jewish Defense Organization, a militant Revisionist Zionist group.

Alan and I found being astray in the woods and having to figure a way out an intellectually stimulating and highly exhilarating pastime. Adding to the excitement was the fact that we never informed our parents about what we were doing, so if we went missing our folks wouldn't have been able to notify the authorities where to look for us. We were independent operators.

One day, as Alan and I were struggling to find a path out of the Prospect Park woodlands, five teenage toughs, who unfortunately just happened to be in the vicinity of where we were blundering around, accosted us. They demanded that we empty our pockets and surrender all we were carrying. Since there were five of them and only two of us and they were bigger than us and had knives, I thought it prudent to obey them; I suspect Alan felt the same way. In any event we both complied with their diktat, except I balked at handing them a pocket watch that I had recently sent away for by mail. I truly loved that timepiece. Though it had cost me only a couple of bucks, I didn't want to part with it because I had tossed away the address to the place where I had ordered it from and didn't know where I could obtain a replacement.

I begged the brigands to let me keep my chronometer, saying that although it was worth next to nothing it had lots of sentimental value to me. I said it was a special birthday present from my grandfather, who was going to take me to a jewelry store to have my initials put on the casing the next time he came over to visit our family. I promised the thugs that if they'd let me retain my pocket watch, they could take everything else I had on me and I would not report the incident to my parents or the police.

One of the bandits said he'd consider my request but first he wanted to inspect my watch, so I gave it over to him. After carefully poring over the object of my affections he returned it to me, telling his friends that it looked kind of cheap to him. However, I was relieved of the rest of the junk I was carrying, namely two dollars, a magnifying glass, a pocketknife, and a package of M&M's. Alan was also stripped of whatever stuff he had with him.

On our way home, Alan and I agreed not to tell our parents that we had been robbed and instead merely to chalk the whole thing up as yet another daring escapade that we'd manage to survive. But my mother found out about it anyway; because she overheard me tell my brother about the affair, which I related to him when I came home after he promised to keep the story a secret.

My mom immediately called the police and two of New York's Finest showed up at our apartment. They asked me to give them descriptions of the guys who had taken Alan's and my property, along with details of the items that were lifted from us. I responded to the best of my ability and threw in the story about how I persuaded the thieves to let me keep my pocket watch. That's an account I probably should have kept to myself, as my mother and the cops lectured me for what seemed like hours about how I should have turned everything over to the muggers because I could have gotten them mad with my pleading and whimpering. "Son," one of the gendarmes said, "your life is more valuable than a silly old watch. If you ever get in a situation like that again, give the crooks what they want. If you don't you may not be as fortunate as you were this time."

I didn't argue with the constable. I simply said, "Thanks for your advice, officer. If I'm ever jumped again I won't put up a fuss. I'll absolutely do whatever I'm told to do." But I was lying. If I ever got into a similar jam again I'd do just what I did before because I believe, as did the 14th-century poet Geoffrey Chaucer, "he that attempts nothing will nothing achieve."

Alan and I stopped going to Prospect Park to get lost in the woods after that attack. We thought we had been fortunate that we were not harmed and we might not be as successful again. Anyway, why take chances? We had had an excellent adventure and lived to tell the tale. For young guys living in the badlands of Brooklyn, you really couldn't do better than that.

The 1950s: Beatniks, Science, and Technology

Beatniks

The term "beatnik" was coined by Herb Caen in an article he published in the *San Francisco Chronicle* in 1958. He devised the name by adding the Russian suffix "nik" to the word "beat." Caen's column launching the expression came out six months after the launch of the Russian space satellite Sputnik and was meant to show that the "beats" and their ideas, like Sputnik, were simply "out of this world."

Beat ideas included a rejection of mainstream American values, experimentation with drugs and alternate forms of sexuality, and an interest in Eastern spirituality. Beat writers such as Jack Kerouac, Allen Ginsberg, and William S. Burroughs spread those notions through their writings. Many consider Kerouac's *On the Road* (1957), a semi-autobiographical, stream-of-consciousness literary endeavor that depicts his mid-century road-trip adventures across the United States and Mexico, the most significant work of the Beat Generation.

In her chronicle *Minor Characters: A Beat Memoir* (1999), Joyce Johnson describes how 1950s American culture co-opted beat philosophy: The "Beat Generation" sold books, sold black turtleneck sweaters and bongos, berets and dark glasses, sold a way of life that seemed like dangerous fun—thus to be either condemned or imitated. Suburban couples could have beatnik parties on Saturday nights and drink too much and fondle each other's wives.

Lots of college students in the 1950s aped the beat mold, with men sporting berets and short pointed beards, rolling their own cigarettes, and playing the bongo drums. Styles for women included wearing black leotards and long, straight, unembellished hair to protest the bourgeois use of beauty parlors. Marijuana use was linked with beat culture and so was Aldous Huxley's *The Doors of Perception* (1954), a book that viewed drugs positively.

Madison Avenue cashed in on the beatnik fad by employing beat terms, like "Daddy-O," "cool man, cool," and "strictly dullsville" in their advertisements. "Hip" record companies used the phrase "Beat Generation" in sales pitches to hawk their new $33^1/_3$-rpm long-playing vinyl records. There was also Rent-a-Beatnik (the ad in the *Village Voice* read "RENT genuine BEATNIKS Badly groomed but brilliant . . ."), *The Beat Generation Cookbook*, and a *MAD* magazine special, featuring mock advertisements for "Paint Smears—all colors, paste on easily" and "Oversize Sweaters for Beatnik chicks—one size only (too big)."

In the entertainment world, the character Maynard G. Krebs, Dobie Gillis's sidekick on the TV series *The Many Loves of Dobie Gillis* (1959-1963), epitomized the beatnik stereotype with his goatee, hip slang, scruffy bohemian appearance, and studious avoidance of anything resembling work, a term Krebs regarded as a four-letter word. Movie director Stanley Donen made fun of beat behavior in his American musical film *Funny Face* (1957). On Broadway, the beat subculture was lampooned in the musical jazz comedy *The Nervous Set* (1959).

During the 1950s, Kerouac spoke out against media typecasting of beats as pseudo-intellectual cartoon-type figures who hung around coffee shops, went to poetry readings, acted like slouches, and used hipster jargon. He argued that being beat was a state of mind that involved living simply and searching for deeper, more meaningful connections to life. That way of thinking emerged big time in the 1960s, with the Beat Generation giving way to the Sixties Counterculture, which was matched by a swing in language from "beatnik" to "hippie."

Science and Technology

Television was just one of many new technologies in the 1950s. In the initial year of that decade, Paper Mate produced the first leak free ballpoint pen (a much-needed advance in an era when people actually wrote letters to each other) and the Haloid Company produced the first photocopy machine. A year later, the first general-purpose electronic computer manufactured for commercial sale, the UNIVAC I, rolled off the assembly line.

In 1952, Edward Teller and his team conducted the first hydrogen bomb test at Eniwetok, an atoll in the South Pacific. The fireball was approximately 3.25 miles wide and the blast created a crater 6,240 feet in diameter and 164 feet deep. The blast and water waves from the explosion, some waves up to 20 feet high, stripped the test islands of all vegetation. The Soviets tested an H-bomb in 1953, boasting that their weapon, unlike the one tested by America, could be dropped from an airplane.

In 1954, the S. W. Farber Company manufactured the first stainless steel electric fry pan and General Electric brought colored kitchen appliances to the market. Goodbye, white! Hello yellow, green, blue, and pink! A two-tone look premiered in the sixties but it never caught on.

In 1955, Zenith engineer Eugene Polley invented the "Flash-Matic," the TV industry's first wireless remote. It was a wonderful invention but the Flash-Matic had trouble working on sunny days, when the sunlight sometimes switched the channels at random. Also in 1955, Dr. Jonas Salk announced the discovery of the polio vaccine, the use of which reduced the worldwide number of polio cases from many hundreds of thousands per year to around a thousand per annum.

The introduction of the commercial videotape recorder in 1956 transformed TV program production. The world's first broadcast via videotape took place on November 30th of that year when CBS Television City in Hollywood played a *Douglas Edwards and the News* program three hours after it had been aired in New York. Time-delayed TV transmission was now a reality.

"Mistake Out," *aka* Liquid Paper, was also unveiled in 1956. Its creator, Dallas secretary Bette Nesmith Graham, used her own kitchen blender to mix up the first batch of Mistake Out. In 1979, the Gillette Corporation bought Liquid Paper from Graham for $47.5 million plus royalties. Besides being an inventor, Graham was the mother of Michael Nesmith, a singer with The Monkees.

On October 4, 1957, the first space satellite was catapulted into the cosmos. A 185-pound Soviet made device, Sputnik I took about an hour and a half to orbit the Earth. A month afterwards, the Soviets launched Sputnik II, an 1,100-pound satellite that carried a live dog, Laika. US scientists moved fast to catch up. In December they fired off Vanguard, which rose four feet off the ground and then exploded. Some reporters labeled Vanguard "Flopnik." A month later Explorer 1 was successfully dispatched and America became a player in the space race.

In 1958, Sweet'N Low was introduced as an artificial sweetener, using saccharin instead of sugar. The name Sweet'N Low derives from an 1863 song by Sir Joseph Barnby, which takes both its title and lyrics from an Alfred Lord Tennyson poem entitled "The Princess: Sweet and Low." Sweet'N Low received US trademark number 1,000,000. Also in 1958: the first domestic jet-airline passenger service was begun by National Airlines between Miami and New York City and temperature-resistant CorningWare debuted.

Pantyhose, a fashion innovation that became a fashion necessity with the arrival of the mini skirt in the 1960s, was brought to the market in 1959. That same year Jack Kilby and Robert Noyce announced another product that has proven to have legs—the microchip, a set of electronic components on a single unit. Fifty years after their first appearance, microchips, *aka* integrated circuits, are found in almost all contemporary electrical devices, including cars, television sets, CD players, and cellular phones. They've become absolutely essential to the modern world—though not as essential as pantyhose is to pantyhose fetishists.

Appendix

What Things Cost in the 1950s
Source: www.tvhistory.tv/1950%20QF.htm

What Things Cost in 1950
Car: $1,750
Gasoline: 27 cents/gal
House: $14,500
Bread: 14 cents/loaf
Milk: 82 cents/gal
Postage Stamp: 3 cents
Stock Market: 235
Average Annual Salary: $3,800
Minimum Wage: 75 cents/hour

What Things Cost in 1951
Car: $1,800
Gasoline: 27 cents/gal
House: $16,000
Bread: 16 cents/loaf
Milk: 92 cents/gal
Postage Stamp: 3 cents
Stock Market: 269
Average Annual Salary: $4,200
Minimum Wage: 75 cents/hour

What Things Cost in 1952
Car: $1,850
Gasoline: 27 cents/gal
House: $17,000
Bread: 16 cents/loaf
Milk: 96 cents/gal
Postage Stamp: 3 cents
Stock Market: 292
Average Annual Salary: $4,500
Minimum Wage: 75 cents/hour

What Things Cost in 1953
Car: $1,850
Gasoline: 29 cents/gal
House: $17,500
Bread: 16 cents/loaf
Milk: 94 cents/gal
Postage Stamp: 3 cents
Stock Market: 281
Average Annual Salary: $4,700
Minimum Wage: 75 cents/hour

What Things Cost in 1954
Car: $1,950
Gasoline: 29 cents/gal
House: $17,500
Bread: 17 cents/loaf
Milk: 92 cents/gal
Postage Stamp: 3 cents
Stock Market: 404
Average Annual Salary: $4,700
Minimum Wage: 75 cents/hour

What Things Cost in 1955
Car: $1,950
Gasoline: 29 cents/gal
House: $17,500
Bread: 18 cents/loaf

Milk: 92 cents/gal
Postage Stamp: 3 cents
Stock Market: 488
Average Annual Salary: $5,000
Minimum Wage: 75 cents/hour

What Things Cost in 1956
Car: $2,100
Gasoline: 30 cents/gal
House: $17,800
Bread: 18 cents/loaf
Milk: 97 cents/gal
Postage Stamp: 3 cents
Stock Market: 499
Average Annual Salary: $5,300
Minimum Wage: $1.00/hour

What Things Cost in 1957
Car: $2,100
Gasoline: 31 cents/gal
House: $18,000
Bread: 19 cents/loaf
Milk: $1.00/gal
Postage Stamp: 3 cents
Stock Market: 436
Average Annual Salary: $5,500
Minimum Wage: $1.00/hour

What Things Cost in 1958
Car: $2,200
Gasoline: 30 cents/gal
House: $18,000
Bread: 19 cents/loaf
Milk: $1.01/gal
Postage Stamp: 4 cents
Stock Market: 584
Average Annual Salary: $5,500
Minimum Wage: $1.00/hour

What Things Cost in 1959
Car: $2,200
Gasoline: 30 cents/gal
House: $18,500
Bread: 20 cents/loaf
Milk: $1.01/gal
Postage Stamp: 4 cents
Stock Market: 679
Average Annual Salary: $5,500
Minimum Wage: $1.00/hour